The New
Brown Bag

Tell Me a Story

The New
Brown Bag

Tell Me a Story
30 Children's Sermons
Based on Best-Loved Books

Phyllis Vos Wezeman
Anna L. Liechty

THE
PILGRIM
PRESS
Cleveland

To Patricia Soltess—whose life story is an "open book" on love
—(P.V.W.)

To Julie Stauffer—
whose love of reading and love of God blesses all the children in her life
—(A.L.L.)

The Pilgrim Press, 700 Prospect Avenue East, Cleveland, Ohio 44115-1100
thepilgrimpress.com

09 08 07 06 05   5 4 3 2 1

Library of Congress Cataloging-in-Publication Data

Wezeman, Phyllis Vos.
    Tell me a story : 30 children's sermons based on best-loved books / Phyllis Vos
Wezeman, Anna L. Liechty.
        p.   cm.   (The new brown bag)
    Includes bibliographical references.
    ISBN 0-8298-1635-6 (pbk. : alk. paper)
    1. Children's sermons.   2. Picture books for children.   3. Church year
sermons.   I. Liechty, Anna L.   II. Title.   IV. Series.

BV4315.W435   2005
252'.53—dc22

2005042987

Contents

Introduction

Everyone loves children's picture books. The illustrations are engaging, the themes are simple, and they speak to the human heart at a basic level, communicating abstract ideas in more concrete and memorable ways. Good preachers and teachers often use stories and their illustrations to introduce important concepts or to summarize and cement essential lessons. Educational research demonstrates the power of metaphor in helping the brain comprehend, organize, and retrieve information. Jesus obviously understood this principle. In his teaching, Jesus communicated with simple, visual messages: "Consider the lilies of the field" (Matthew 6:28), or "If you had faith the size of a mustard seed" (Luke 17:6), or "No one after lighting a lamp puts it under the bushel basket" (Matthew 5:15). The parables and teachings of Jesus speak to the heart by appealing to our senses—just like children's picture books do today.

The lessons we learn from Scripture are important and stay with us; however, sometimes we have heard the stories so often, they become too familiar. We have them memorized, but not internalized. To address this need, pastors and teachers must continue to look for fresh ways to retell biblical truths, to revisit the themes of the church year, and to link celebrations found in the secular calendar with the message of faith. What better way to refresh listeners and build connections than with children's picture books?

While many Christian leaders and educators have used children's literature with groups, no resource has been available to connect published titles and authors with religious instructional purposes, let alone to provide suggestions for a weekly children's message using a concrete teaching tool. This resource provides readers with all of the necessary information to identify picture books and appropriate their message for use in the church. The contents found in *Tell Me a Story: 30 Children's Sermons Based on Best-Loved Books* will empower leaders to use children's literature to reach people of all ages, surprising them with entertaining, engaging, and inspiring stories taken from today's bookshelves, but transporting hearts back to the message first heard at the feet of Jesus.

Overview

What is this book?

Tell Me a Story: 30 Children's Sermons Based on Best-Loved Books is a collection of messages primarily designed for use with kindergarten through upper-elementary youth. This resource addresses the special days and holidays of the liturgical and secular calendars from a variety of approaches. While each sermon is based on a scripture passage or verse, the message also incorporates a popular children's picture book to communicate the central theme.

Each message uses a consistent format based on the following components:

PASSAGE: Each sermon is based on a specific scripture text, which is listed for reference.

PURPOSE: Each message's central theme is summarized in one simple statement.

PREPARATION: A complete bibliographical entry, as well as a short summary of the story, is given for the children's book featured in each sermon. While it would be helpful to use each book's illustrations in connection with the children's sermon, it is not necessary to have a copy of the book to share the message.

A suggestion for a teaching tool for each object lesson is provided and, if needed, instructions are outlined.

PRESENTATION: A complete script for an interactive dialogue with the children is offered.

PRAYER: A brief prayer, suitable for repetition by the children, is given as a summary statement of the message.

Although the thirty sermons are listed by title in the contents at the beginning of the book, a significant component of this collection is the Resource Section at the end which cross-references all entries by

Children's Book titles, Scripture Passages, and Teaching Tools.

Why is this book needed?

This book—a ready-to-use collection of messages to help children explore various aspects of the church year and the calendar year—is unique. Since these special days and holidays are celebrated on an annual basis, church leaders must continue to find fresh approaches to familiar stories and themes. This material provides an opportunity for the teacher, pastor, or parent to expand their available resources. Although there are books of children's sermons that address the seasons, there is nothing that connects the more familiar world of children's literature with the intangible world of liturgy and cycles. This resource provides an extremely helpful reference allowing readers to find ways to make connections between the common events of life and the relevance of the church's message. The use of picture books and tangible teaching tools also allows children to review and make meaning from the illustrations, as well as facilitating their intellectual growth from abstract to concrete thinking.

Who will use this book?

This book will be used in congregations by clergypersons, Christian education directors, church school teachers, children's church coordinators, mid-week programmers, and special project leaders; in parochial schools by administrators and teachers; and in homes by parents and grandparents.

Messages are designed for children in kindergarten through grade five but are adaptable for boys and girls in preschool and young people in middle grades. They will also be appreciated by adults of all ages and appropriate for intergenerational audiences.

How will this book be most helpful?

In congregations, this collection will be used as children's sermons in worship, homilies in children's church, messages in church school classes, reflections in mid-week ministries, meditations in youth groups, and devotions at church camp. They will also be useful as lessons in confirmation classes and religious education programs. In Christian schools, they will be used in chapel services and classroom talks. In families, they will be helpful as a focus for mealtime devotions, faith formation, and bedtime stories.

1

Envisioned as One: New Year's Day
Old Turtle

PASSAGE: Revelation 21:5

PURPOSE: As the New Year begins, we acknowledge that only God can bring about unity in the world, and only when humans listen for God's presence.

PREPARATION: Children's Book
Old Turtle. by Douglas Wood; watercolors by Cheng-Khee Chee. Duluth, Minnesota: Pfeifer-Hamilton, 1992.

Book Summary: When all of creation—ants, fish, sky, stones, trees—begin arguing over who or what God is, quiet Old Turtle is the only one who has the wisdom and the ability to see beyond herself to capture the essence of God's vision.

TEACHING TOOL: Calendar

PRESENTATION:
What is this? (*Hold up a calendar for the New Year and wait for an answer.*) Which number goes best with this calendar: 12, 365, 52, 7, or 30? How many vote for the number 12? (*Repeat voting for each number. If time permits, let each person argue why he or she would choose that number over the others.*) You all have good reasons for your choices. There are 12 months in a calendar year, 365 days, 52

weeks, 7 days in a week, and 30 days in almost all the months. So you disagreed, but with good reasons. That reminds me of a story about God.

In the book *Old Turtle*, Douglas Wood tells a tale about creation and Cheng-Khee Chee provides watercolor illustrations that help us envision the beautiful world God made and all the creatures in it. In the story, we learn that in the beginning of time all the parts of creation believed that God was just like them—the stones thought that God was a rock that never moved; the stars said that God was a faraway twinkling; the ant said that God was a feeling very near; the river said that God was a force that moved through the heart of things. Old Turtle listened to each part of creation's argument about God as their voices became louder and louder, until, finally, Old Turtle explained that God was all of these things: deep like the ocean, high like the mountain, and silent like the giant rock. Old Turtle explained that God was going to add one final creation that would help everyone remember who God is and how to reflect God's many gifts. Can you guess who or what was that final creation? Humans! But guess what—humans forgot. They began to argue, to hate, and to kill, until they had almost destroyed creation and one another because they could not remember who they were or who God was. Then the voices of creation spoke: the mountain suggested that God was in the ocean, the faraway star declared that God was very close, until finally human beings began to listen and to see God in one another. Then Old Turtle smiled—and so did God.

As the New Year begins, we can decide to stop arguing about who is right. We can look at the calendar and remember that even though it has many different parts, it is still ONE year. We can become wise like the people finally do in the *Old Turtle* story and begin to see ONE God in all creation. We envision God as One, even though all things reflect God's nature. When we begin to listen for God's presence, then we come closer to God's vision for us to be one, as well.

PRAYER:
Dear God, thank you for the many beauties of creation. In the New Year, help us to listen for your presence in the earth and to see your love in one another. Amen.

2
Touched by Light: Epiphany

Three Wise Women

PASSAGE: Isaiah 9:2b

PURPOSE: The light of Epiphany reveals that Christ came for everyone who seeks the light of truth.

PREPARATION: Children's Book
Three Wise Women. by Mary Hoffman; pictures by Lynne Russell, Illustrator. New York: Phyllis Fogelman Books, 1999.

Book Summary: Three wise women follow a bright star to find a very special newborn baby in a stable, where each of them is able in her own way to give the child a gift.

TEACHING TOOL: Star

PRESENTATION:

Do you recognize this shape? *(Hold up a star.)* Of course, it's a star! We know the star as an important symbol of Christmas that shone above the manger where Jesus was born. Did you know that the star is also the symbol of the next season of the church year—Epiphany? Epiphany means "revelation." The star revealed not only where Jesus was in Bethlehem, the light of the star also guided people from far-away to seek the newborn king. Who were they? *(Wait for someone to volunteer "the three wise men.")* Yes, the Magi saw the special star as a sign of God's involvement in something new and wonderful.

One book written about the Star of Bethlehem is called *Three Wise Women*. Wait a minute you say. There were three wise men. There weren't three wise women! Well, that's true—not that the Bible writes about specifically, at least. Mary Hoffman, the author, and Lynne Russell, the illustrator, added to the story from the Bible. In their version, three women—one from the West baking bread, one from the South comforting her child, and an old woman from the Southeast telling stories to her grandchildren—look up to see the Christmas star. They are attracted to the light and miraculously find their way to the Christ child just as the Magi are leaving. The women are drawn to the Babe in the manger, but don't have mighty gifts to present like the wise men. Instead, they offer the gifts they possess—fresh-baked bread, a charming story, and a child's sweet kiss.

Our star is not real, and yet it can teach us about real stars. *(Hold up the star.)* The story *Three Wise Women* may not actually be true, but the story tells the truth. The revelation—or epiphany—that the story brings is that Christ came to break bread with us, Christ came to share stories that teach God's truth, and Christ came to reveal that love is the most powerful force in the whole world.

PRAYER:

Dear God, thank you for revealing your love to us by sending Jesus. Help us to offer the gifts we have to others in Christ's name. Amen.

3
Spoken with Love:
Valentine's Day
I'll Always Love You

PASSAGE: 1 John 4:7

PURPOSE: When we express our love every day, we experience God's perfect presence and live with no regrets.

PREPARATION: Children's Book
I'll Always Love You. by Hans Wilhelm; New York: Crown, 1985.

Book Summary: *I'll Always Love You* tells the story of a young child's love for his dog through all the stages of the pet's life. He recounts their shared experiences, and remembers that every night he told Elfie, "I'll always love you." Elfie ages and ultimately dies, but the young boy's sadness is tempered by his knowledge that he had fully expressed his love in both word and deed.

TEACHING TOOL: Heart-shaped Valentine card

PRESENTATION:

I'd guess that some of you have made cards shaped like this, right? *(Hold up the heart-shaped Valentine card.)* Why do we share this kind of greeting? *(Let someone suggest that a heart stands for love, which is the message of Valentine's Day.)* Yes, Valentine's Day is a holiday when we are supposed to tell the people important to us that we love them—or at least like them a lot. Is it important to tell people that we care about them? I think so!

Do you know the story, *I'll Always Love You?* How many of you have pets? This story is about a boy and his dog named Elfie. The young boy tells about growing up with Elfie, who was his dog, not his brother's or sister's pet. The two share a very special relationship. Every night the boy tells Elfie, "I'll always love you." And he did. They played together, slept together, and grew older together. Of course, dogs don't live as long as most people do; so the story explains that the time comes for Elfie to die. That seems a sad message for Valentine's Day, doesn't it? However, the boy explains that—even though he was very sad when Elfie died—he felt very glad that Elfie knew how much he was loved. The boy had no regrets like some other members of his family who were sad that they had not spoken of their love for the dog.

The point is that we have an opportunity every day, not only on Valentine's Day, to tell those we care about how much they mean to us. Like the young boy, we want to live expressing our love every day. That may seem like a challenge, but in the church we understand that this is the way God loves us. God's message for us is the same: "I'll always love you." We can listen for God's words of love in many ways: in the Bible, in the sunrise, in the hymns we sing in church. But most of all, God speaks to us through the words and actions of people who know and love God. In a way, we become God's valentines to others. Because we know that God always loves us, we have love that overflows from our lives into the lives of other people who may not have gotten the message yet. So, open your heart, and share the Good News: God loves you—and so do I!

PRAYER:
Dear God, thank you for the overflowing love you pour into our hearts. Help us to share the message that you always love us, no matter what. Amen.

4

Reminded to Forgive:
First Sunday in Lent
*What If The Zebras Lost
Their Stripes?*

PASSAGE: Romans 3:21–24

PURPOSE: We begin our Lenten journey by acknowledging everyone's need for God's forgiveness.

PREPARATION: Children's Book
What If The Zebras Lost Their Stripes? by John Reitano; illustrated by William Haines. New York: Paulist Press, 1998.

Summary: *What If The Zebras Lost Their Stripes?* questions what would happen if some zebras lost white stripes and were only black and some lost black stripes and were only white. Would zebras begin to fight with one another and stop living life as loving friends? Surely, zebras would be smarter than to let their colors tear them apart.

TEACHING TOOL: Striped paper or material

PRESENTATION:
(Hold up the paper or fabric.) Tell me, is this white material with black stripes or black material with white stripes? *(Pause for speculation.)* We really can't tell, can we? We just know that it's black and white striped material—just like a zebra is a black and white striped

creature. Have you ever read the book *What If The Zebras Lost Their Stripes?* The story asks us to think about what would happen if some zebras lost white stripes and turned black and some lost black stripes and turned white. Do you suppose they might not recognize each other as zebras anymore? Would they begin to fight and forget that they were friends? The book suggests that maybe God made zebras so there would be no black or white—only stripes!

On this first Sunday in Lent, we are beginning our journey to Easter. One of the ways we prepare during Lent is to search our hearts for answers to important questions. For example, we might ask ourselves, "How do I treat other people?" Or, more importantly, "How does God want me to treat other people?" Sometimes we human beings act like zebras who have lost our stripes. We look at others and see them as different from ourselves. We might be tempted to make fun, be unkind, or even fight with others who "aren't like us." It's hard to understand why we act that way sometimes, but the Bible offers us some reasons and some ways to find God's plan for living.

As Lent begins, we read Bible passages that remind us that ever since the first people, Adam and Eve, there has been a big problem in the world. It's called "sin." We human beings tend to forget God, and we forget to live in the love and harmony that God's people should have for each other. One of the opportunities we have in Lent is to remember that we are all sinners—just like zebras are all zebras, whether they have black stripes or white ones. As sinful people, we must all turn to God because God is the only one who can forgive our sin and help us to live in love and friendship with the other people on our planet. If we recognize that everyone needs God's love and forgiveness, then we understand that we are really all just alike. We are sinful people who have to turn to our loving Creator each and every day—not only during Lent, but all year long.

PRAYER:
Dear God, forgive us each day for the times we forget to follow your ways. Help us to forgive one another just as you forgive each one of us. Amen.

5

Empowered to Share:
Second Sunday in Lent
Benjamin Brody's Backyard Bag

PASSAGE: 1 Peter 2:21

PURPOSE: During Lent we are challenged to reflect on what it means to be a follower of Jesus.

PREPARATION: Children's Book
Benjamin Brody's Backyard Bag. by Phyllis Vos Wezeman and Colleen Aalsburg Wiessner. Illustrated by Christopher Raschka. Elgin, IL: Brethren Press, 1991.

Book Summary: Benjamin Brody's playful experiment to discover uses for an empty paper shopping bag leads him to an informative encounter with a woman who uses a bag as her home.

TEACHING TOOL: Paper shopping bag

PRESENTATION:
How many of you have a place at home where you store extra bags like this one? (*Wait for show of hands or responses.*) I have a place where I save bags like these because you never know when you might need something to help you carry or store things. Suppose that you could only own what you could carry in a bag like this. In

the story called *Benjamin Brody's Backyard Bag*, by Phyllis Wezeman and Colleen Wiessner, a little boy wants a bag to carry like the rest of his family. His backpack is worn out and he doesn't have anything important like a briefcase or a school bag. All he gets to use is an empty paper shopping bag. But Benjamin is an inventive little kid. He discovers lots of uses for his brown bag like a garage for his cars, a tablecloth for a picnic, and a container for his rock collection.

When Benjamin and his mother go for a walk with his baby sister, he meets a lady who also uses a bag to collect useful and interesting things. Only Benjamin discovers that the bag contains everything the woman owns. The bag is really her home. Benjamin is surprised and thoughtful as he realizes for the first time what it means to be homeless. Even though she has little, the "bag lady" shares one of her treasures with Benjamin. On his way home, Benjamin asks his mother what they can do to help the woman. Benjamin's mother suggests one more use for his brown bag—to make a list of ways they could help homeless people. By the time he returns to his own home, Benjamin's bag has helped him learn a great deal, and he feels like his simple brown paper shopping bag is the best container of all.

During Lent, we are challenged to reflect on what it means to be a follower of Jesus. We know that all of us are sinners and depend upon God for forgiveness and hope. However, like Benjamin, we must also learn that God needs us to use whatever we have at our disposal to make a difference for other people in God's world. Sometimes we may feel like who we are and what we have isn't much, but that's not the message of Lent. On earth, Jesus didn't have wealth or power or impressive friends. Instead, he used the simple elements of life—fish, bread, grapes, mud, wind, and seas—to make a difference in people's lives, to help them come to know God's love and care. Like Benjamin, we must use what we have and be willing to care about whomever God brings into our lives. If we are going to follow Jesus, then caring about other people has to be "our bag."

PRAYER:
Dear God, thank you for opportunities to make a difference in the lives of other people. Help us to be alert and inventive so that we may use whatever we have to bless those in need. Amen.

6

Freed to Love:
Third Sunday in Lent
The Selfish Giant

Passage: Ephesians 2:14

Purpose: During Lent we remember that Christ's deeds of love free us to open our lives to one another.

Preparation: Children's Book
Oscar Wilde's The Selfish Giant. Retold by Fiona Waters. Illustrated by Fabian Negrin. New York: Knopf, 2000.

Book Summary: A once selfish giant welcomes the children to his previously forbidden garden and is eventually rewarded by a little child he had once befriended.

Teaching Tool: Spring plant in full bloom

Presentation:

Isn't this a beautiful spring plant? *(Display the blooming spring plant.)* Everyone loves the beautiful plants of springtime! Isn't it exciting when spring comes to the earth and gardens burst into bloom? During the season of Lent spring comes to North America, and we enjoy the colorful delights of plants like this one. Wouldn't it be sad if spring never arrived? If, instead, our gardens stayed locked in ice and cold with no flowers or budding trees? In the story *The Selfish Giant*, by Oscar Wilde, that is exactly what happens to the selfish giant's garden when he builds a high wall and forbids the children to run and play among his flowers and trees. Winter comes and stays until he realizes that what he tries to keep only for himself can no longer bring him happiness.

The giant repents of his selfishness and helps a small boy into one of his trees. With his act of gentleness and sharing, spring returns fully to the garden. Then the giant knocks down the wall so that the children can visit and play. However, the giant—who is no longer selfish—cannot find the little boy he first helped. In fact he doesn't see him anymore until the giant has become an old man, one who is loved very much by the children who come to play among the flowers' and trees, especially in the springtime. At the end of the story, when the giant sees the boy again, he discovers the child carries wounds in his hands and feet—the wounds of love he is told. The child offers to take the unselfish giant to paradise where it is always beautiful.

Does the little boy with the wounds of love remind you of someone? *(Wait for someone to suggest "Jesus.")* Yes, the little boy in the story seems to symbolize the love of Christ who came to earth, suffered, and died for the sins of people. Now, Christ offers eternal life to those who follow God's ways. Like the giant, we must learn to break down the walls of selfishness and look for opportunities to reach out to others. During Lent, we remember what Jesus came to earth to do. We remember the lessons Jesus came to earth to teach. And we remember that we must open our hearts and change, just like the giant who decided not to be selfish anymore.

PRAYER:

Dear God, thank you for helping us to take down the walls of selfishness. Show us how to live so that we can share your love with everyone. Amen.

7
Justified by Faith:
Fourth Sunday in Lent
The Spyglass

PASSAGE: 2 Corinthians 5:7

PURPOSE: During Lent we are challenged to look at life through the eyes of faith to discover God's vision for our lives.

PREPARATION: Children's Book
The Spyglass: A Story of Faith. Richard Paul Evans; Illustrated by Jonathan Linton. New York: Simon & Schuster Books for Young Readers, 2000.

Book Summary: The inhabitants of a kingdom that has fallen on hard times discover the value of faith when they learn to consider what might be and labor to make it so.

TEACHING TOOL: Spyglass

PRESENTATION:
Have you ever looked through a spyglass before? (*Hold up the spyglass, but look through the wrong end.*) That's funny, I thought the spyglass was supposed to make things far away look closer? This spyglass doesn't work at all! (*Wait for suggestions to turn the glass around.*) What? I need to look through the small end? Oh! Yes, that is much

better! Wow! Now I can see everything far away! (*If time permits, share the spyglass to allow all to have a look.*) Did you ever consider that a spyglass could be a symbol of faith?

In the story called *The Spyglass*, by Richard Paul Evans, a kingdom is suffering because it has lost all of its greatness. Everything from the king's castle to each farmer's field is in disrepair. The king and the people live sad, empty lives until an old beggar with a spyglass comes to visit the king. In exchange for his supper, he offers to loan the king his spyglass. When the king looks through the spyglass—at the right end—he sees beautiful farms and prosperous villages. The beggar tells the king that he has only seen what could be so, and seeing must come before doing. "Now go and make it so," the beggar instructs the king. As the king shares the vision through the spyglass with the others in his kingdom, they, too, begin to work to create the vision the spyglass reveals. When the beggar returns, the kingdom has changed. The people have changed. All because they caught a glimpse of what was possible and worked to make it happen.

Lent is a time for us to look through the spyglass of faith. Faith can show us what great things are possible. We can catch a glimpse of the person God calls us to be. Like in the story, seeing comes before doing. Lent is our opportunity to focus on faith. (*Hold up the spyglass, first the wrong way, then correctly.*) If our faith is focused on the life of Jesus, we discover the vision of what our lives can be. Then we will be ready to "go and make it so."

PRAYER:
Dear God, give us the vision of faith to see what our church and our lives can become. Then help us to get to work to make your vision a reality. Amen.

8

Given with Joy:
Fifth Sunday in Lent
Miss Fannie's Hat

PASSAGE: Hebrews 12:2

PURPOSE: During Lent we look to the pattern of Jesus' sacrifice and discover that selfless giving is the secret to a life filled with joy.

PREPARATION: Children's Book
Miss Fannie's Hat. Jan Karon; Illustrated by Toni Goffe. Minneapolis, MN: Augsburg 1998.

Book Summary: When ninety-nine-year-old Miss Fannie gives up her favorite pink straw hat with the roses to help raise money for her church, she receives an unexpected reward.

TEACHING TOOL: Pink straw hat with pink roses

PRESENTATION:
How do you like my hat? (*Model, or have someone model, the hat and invite comments.*) In the not too distant past, women never went anywhere important without wearing a fancy hat. If you were getting dressed up, a hat was a must. Because they are a vanishing tradition, some of those hats are quite valuable. Some folks today collect antique hats; and sometimes those "old" headpieces bring high prices in sales and auctions.

In the story *Miss Fannie's Hat*, author Jan Karon celebrates just such an event. Miss Fannie was a ninety-nine-year-old lady with a lifetime collection of beautiful hats. She wore her favorite hat—the pink one with roses—every Easter Sunday for thirty-five years. It was an important part of springtime for her congregation, and everyone admired the beautiful straw hat that sat atop Miss Fannie's cloud of soft gray hair. When her church was having an auction in the hopes of raising much-needed money to make repairs, Miss Fannie talked to God about which hat she might offer for the church to put up for bidding. Miss Fannie began to think about what kinds of great changes could come from money her hat might fetch—and she decided to give her favorite one. Soon, instead of thinking about the sacrifice of losing her favorite hat, she was excited about what she could help make happen with her gift. Sure enough, Miss Fannie's straw hat with pink roses inspired lots of bids and raised the funds to help her church fix the organ and patch the bell. When the next Easter came, Miss Fannie headed to worship without wearing a hat at all. But guess what—there was one more improvement that the money from Miss Fannie's hat provided her little church—dozens of pink rose bushes were planted in and around the yard. Everyone thought the church looked just like Miss Fannie's favorite hat.

Miss Fannie understood an important idea about Jesus that we remember during Lent. Jesus sacrificed what was most precious of all to make a difference for human beings. Jesus embraced the cross and offered his life for each of us. What could possibly be more precious to give than your own life? Lent is a time in the church year when we learn that a sacrifice of love is not a sad and mournful event. Instead, giving of ourselves to help others is the secret to the greatest joy of all. When we discover—with God's help—what we are called to give for others, then our lives burst into bloom with the joy of God's goodness and become just about as bright and cheerful as Miss Fannie's hat.

PRAYER:
Dear God, we are grateful that Jesus sacrificed his life for us. Help us to find the joy that comes from caring more for people than for things. Amen.

9
Offered in Love: Palm/Passion Sunday, Sixth Sunday in Lent
The Giving Tree

Passage: Ephesians 5:2

Purpose: Christ offers his extreme love for us even though we may not understand or appreciate his sacrifice.

Preparation: Children's Book
The Giving Tree. Shel Silverstein. New York: Harper and Row, 1964.

Book Summary: A young boy grows to manhood and old age experiencing the love and generosity of a tree that gives to him without thought of return.

Teaching Tool: Palm branches

Presentation:

Hooray for Palm Sunday! *(Hold up palm branches and wave them in the air.)* This is a great day for a parade, right? What is Palm Sunday all about? *(Let a volunteer tell the story of Jesus' entrance to Jerusalem. Prompt or guide as necessary.)* Yes, Palm Sunday is about Jesus riding into Jerusalem and being loved and worshiped by the crowd. Everyone was so excited to see him that they cut down branches from the trees and waved them in the air, or laid them on the dusty road to make a path for Jesus and his little donkey. Have you ever wondered why the crowd was so excited to see Jesus on Sunday, but by Friday they were calling for him to be crucified? There's a story that might help us understand; it's called *The Giving Tree* by Shel Silverstein.

In this story, a little boy delights in playing in the shade of a wonderful tree, gathering her leaves to make himself a crown, climbing her trunk and swinging from her branches, even eating the apples she produced. The tree loved the boy and the boy loved the tree. But as time went by, the boy grew older. He didn't find pleasure in simply enjoying the tree; instead he wanted things from the tree—like money. The tree offered the boy her apples to sell to get money so that he would be happy. The tree willingly gave the apples and the boy carried them away. After a long time, the boy came back to the tree, but he was too busy to climb and play. Instead he wanted a house so that he could have a wife and children. The tree offered the boy his branches to build a house, so the boy cut off the tree's branches and went away to build his house. Again, after a long while, the boy returned—still unhappy. This time he wanted to go far, far away. He asked the tree for a boat. The tree offered her trunk for the boy to make a boat so he could sail away. By the time the boy returned from his trip, he was an old man. "I'm sorry," the stump of the tree said, "I have nothing more to give you." But the boy was too old to climb or eat apples; all he wanted was a place to rest. And that, the tree could offer him. At last, both the boy and the tree were happy.

The Giving Tree is a sad story. We wonder why the boy doesn't see how badly he is treating the tree that loves him so much. He is simply too selfish. That's exactly what was wrong with the crowd on Palm Sunday. They wanted Jesus to come into Jerusalem and kick out the Romans and become their earthly king. Jesus, however, offered them an even better kingdom—a heavenly realm where they might live forever with God. In their selfishness, they were angry because they did not receive just what they wanted. So, by Friday, the crowd shouted, "Crucify him!" If we think of Jesus' sacrifice on the cross, we can understand what *The Giving Tree* really means. From the tree of the cross, Jesus looked on the crowd gathered and asked God to forgive them, for they didn't know what they were doing. We can be like the boy in the story and take Jesus' loving sacrifice for granted.

Or we can learn to rest quietly at the foot of the cross, and to find true happiness on earth in Jesus' love.

PRAYER:

Dear God, forgive us when we forget to be grateful for all you have given us. Help us to remember that Jesus died for us and to remember how much we are loved. Amen.

10
Helped to Remember: Maundy Thursday
Wilfrid Gordon McDonald Partridge

PASSAGE: Luke 22:19–20

PURPOSE: On Maundy Thursday we recall the significance of the gift of remembering.

PREPARATION: Children's Book
Wilfrid Gordon McDonald Partridge. Mem Fox; Illustrated by Julie Vivas. Brooklyn, NY: Kane/Miller, 1985.

Book Summary: A small boy tries to discover the meaning of "memory" so he can help an elderly friend who has lost her ability to remember.

TEACHING TOOLS: Basket containing an egg, a football, a marionette, a medal, a seashell, a Communion cup, and a loaf of bread

---

PRESENTATION:

Once there was a young boy named Wilfrid Gordon McDonald Partridge whose favorite friend lived next door in a home for old people. She had four names, too: Nancy Alison Delacourt Cooper, but Wilfrid called her "Miss Nancy." One day Wilfrid overheard his parents pitying Miss Nancy because she had lost her memory. He visited several people at the old folk's home and asked them "What's a memory?" One person said a memory was something warm. Another said it was something from long ago. Others said it was something that makes you cry or something that makes you laugh. Finally, someone told Wilfrid that a memory is something as precious as gold. Because Miss Nancy had lost her own memory, Wilfrid wanted to help her find it by sharing some of his own. He gathered items in a basket to take to Miss Nancy. *(Hold up each item from the basket during the explanation.)* There was an egg that was warm; a seashell he had found long ago; his grandfather's medal, remembered with sadness; a puppet on strings that made him laugh; and his very own football, as precious as gold. As Miss Nancy explored the items in Wilfrid's basket, she began to remember—a bird's nest *(egg)*, a trip to the beach *(seashell)*, her brother who left for the war *(medal)*, her sister's laughter *(puppet)*, and playing catch with Wilfrid *(football)*. Thanks to a very small boy, Miss Nancy found her memory again.

Wilfrid Gordon McDonald Partridge is a wonderful story about making memories and sharing memories with those we love. There is a celebration in the church year that has the same meaning. That celebration occurs on the Thursday before Easter, called Maundy Thursday. Maundy means "commandment of God"—which suggests that the day is very important, one we should remember. In fact, that is what we are supposed to do on Maundy Thursday—we are supposed to remember the Last Supper that Jesus shared with his disciples. Jesus gave his disciples simple objects to help them—and us—remember: a loaf of bread and a cup of juice or wine. *(Hold up the symbols.)* Just like Miss Nancy could remember when she held Wilfrid's gifts, Jesus helps us to remember that he offered his life for us—his body is the bread; his blood is the juice or wine. Jesus also knew that we humans would be likely to forget. However, if we share warm, simple memories with one another, we experience God's love and renew our relationships. That's the message of *Wilfrid Gordon McDonald Partridge*, and that is the message of Maundy Thursday. When we share the memory of Jesus' meal and follow Christ's commandment that we remember what he has done for us, we discover that we have important friends, both the ones who receive the meal with us, and the One who gives us the reason to remember, our best friend, Jesus.

PRAYER:

Dear God, thank you for the simple gifts that help us understand what Jesus means to us. Help us to remember Christ's love for us each time we share this special meal. Amen.

11

Lent

Fulfilled with Purpose: Good Friday

The Tale of Three Trees

PASSAGE: John 3:17

PURPOSE: On Good Friday, God's purpose in sending Jesus is fulfilled, securing salvation for all who believe.

PREPARATION: Children's Book
The Tale of Three Trees: A Traditional Folktale. Retold by Angela Elwell Hunt; Illustrated by Tim Jonke. Colorado Springs, CO: Lion Publishing, 1989.

Book Summary: Once upon a mountaintop, three little trees stood and dreamed of what they wanted to become when they grew up. Each of their dreams comes true in an unexpected way.

TEACHING TOOL: A piece of lumber

PRESENTATION:

What do you see? *(Hold up a piece of lumber.)* Wood? Is that all you see? If you could look with a carpenter's eye, you might be able to see a beautiful leg for a table, a carefully fashioned wooden box, or a million toothpicks! If you were a Cub Scout, you might see a Pinewood

Derby car! Those who have the vision can look at a piece of wood and see possibilities.

Do you know the story called *The Tale of Three Trees*? This traditional folktale tells of three little trees that have big dreams. One longs to be made into a beautiful treasure chest; another imagines that it will be a great ship. The third hopes to remain high on the mountain and point the way to God. One day three woodcutters come and take down all three trees. The first becomes a feedbox for animals; the second is crafted into a simple fishing boat instead of a great ship. The third is simply stripped into beams and left in the lumberyard. It appears that none of their dreams have come true. However, the feedbox actually becomes the manger in which Mary lays the treasure of the newborn child. The simple fishing boat experiences the power of Jesus as he quiets the storm. The beams of the third tree are formed into the cross that Jesus must carry; and so, in fact, the tree does point the way to God. On Good Friday we remember Jesus' death on that cross. The day seems far from good when we remember Christ's suffering and sacrifice. However, God's vision extends beyond what we can see on earth. Like the three trees who finally understood that their dreams had been granted in ways they could not imagine, we can understand that this day is "good" because Jesus brings us victory over death. Like a carpenter sees the possibilities that lie within the wood, Jesus offers his life because he sees the potential in each one of us. With faith in Christ, we find meaning and purpose so that our lives can become something beautiful for God. Like the three trees, we can dare to dream and trust in God who can even turn death into life.

PRAYER:
Dear God, thank you for the goodness you can bring even to impossible situations. Help us to trust your vision for our lives. Amen.

12
Awakened to New Life: Easter Sunday
The Very Hungry Caterpillar

PASSAGE: 1 Corinthians 15:51

PURPOSE: We can recognize the message of Easter in the miracle of metamorphosis.

PREPARATION: Children's Book
The Very Hungry Caterpillar. Eric Carle. New York: Philomel Books, 1983.

Book Summary: *The Very Hungry Caterpillar* follows the progress of a hungry little caterpillar as he eats his way through a varied and very large quantity of food until, full at last, he forms a cocoon around himself and goes to sleep only to awake changed into a beautiful butterfly.

TEACHING TOOL: Book, model, or poster of the life cycle of a butterfly

---

PRESENTATION:
Happy Easter! What a wonderful celebration we share on Easter Sunday! Does anyone know why the church is so joyful on Easter? *(Allow someone to share the message that Jesus rose from the dead.)* Yes! That is the good news of this day: Jesus is not dead. He is risen as he promised! As Christians we follow a living Savior, and Easter is our

day to celebrate Christ's resurrection. It almost seems too wonderful to believe, right? Jesus was crucified and buried. How could he possibly be raised from the dead? Of course, by faith we believe and accept the Bible's message passed down to us from those first disciples who saw Jesus with their own eyes on Easter morning. But God also gives us the opportunity to find faith in even more ways! God gives us the opportunity to witness transforming power in the world around us.

Do you know the stages in the life cycle of a butterfly? (*Hold up the book, model, or poster of the stages and point out the changes.*) Many stories have been written about the wondrous changes called "metamorphosis." One of the most familiar stories is called *The Very Hungry Caterpillar.* (*If the listeners know the story, consider having them recount it.*) We follow the story of the very hungry caterpillar from the little egg on a leaf in the moonlight through all of his changes. He hatches out and begins to eat, and eat, and eat! When he is finally full, the little caterpillar has grown quite large, and he goes to sleep inside the cocoon he built for himself. The caterpillar has disappeared; but, in a few weeks, he chews his way out. And, guess what? He is changed! The big, fat caterpillar has become a beautiful butterfly! That's an amazing change! It doesn't even seem possible, but many of us have seen that change with our own eyes. The message of *The Very Hungry Caterpillar* reminds us that miracles are all around us and nothing is too hard for God.

So on Easter Sunday we often use butterflies as symbols of new life. Easter's message gives us hope even though death is a reality in our world. Our hope comes from Jesus' resurrection. When Jesus died, he offered his life for us, and he trusted God to make something beautiful out of his suffering and pain. And, guess what? God did! Now we know that death is not the end. Faith in Jesus means that in death, like the caterpillar in the cocoon, we are transformed so that, like Jesus, we are raised to new life with God. Imagine how truly beautiful that must be!

PRAYER:

Dear God, thank you for the message of hope we find in the world around us and especially on Easter Sunday. Help us to place our faith in Jesus so that we can find new life. Amen.

13
Nurtured to Grow: Mother's Day
Stellaluna

PASSAGE: Proverbs 22:6

PURPOSE: The family of faith nurtures future generations in the law of love.

PREPARATION: Children's Book
Stellaluna. Janell Cannon. San Diego, CA: Harcourt Brace Jovanovich, 1993.

Book Summary: After she falls headfirst into a bird's nest, a baby bat is raised like a bird until she is reunited with her birth mother.

TEACHING TOOL: Bat Finger Puppet

PRESENTATION:
Do you like bats? *(Hold up the bat puppet.)* Bats are really important insect-eating mammals that we should try to appreciate. Do you know the story of *Stellaluna*, by Janell Cannon, about the little bat that was raised as a bird? When Stellaluna was very young her mother was attacked by an owl. Because Stellaluna couldn't fly very far, she falls into a nest with baby birds. Her feathery foster mother feeds Stellaluna fat, green grasshoppers that the little bat finds disgusting. However, if she wants to eat, she has to take what her new family has to offer. Stellaluna also gets in trouble for teaching her stepbrothers and stepsisters to hang upside down outside their nest.

The mother bird insists that all her young ones stay safely inside the nest. Obediently, Stellaluna learns to follow the rules for birds, and she lives and grows, trying hard to be a good bird, even though she is unable to land gracefully on a tree branch, and she never learns to like grasshoppers.

One day, Stellaluna flies ahead and doesn't hear her family say it's time to turn around and fly home. Instead, she gets lost, finds a tree, and tries to hang right side up by her thumbs for the night. In the dark, her original family finds her and Stellaluna is reunited with her mother. Stellaluna is delighted to learn that she is not clumsy and that there are foods like fruit that she finds delightful. However, Stellaluna cannot forget her foster family. Even though they are different, the love they share for each other is the same.

Stellaluna is a wonderful story for Mother's Day because we can learn some very important lessons about nurturing. Most people hold a special place in their hearts for their mothers. Stellaluna must have been very sad when she and her mother were separated. However, God can provide the love and care we need to live in many ways. Just like the birds accepted and nurtured Stellaluna, there are families who adopt or take in foster children. Some have stepmothers who make room in their homes and in their hearts to love and care for a "new" family. On Mother's Day, we can thank God for all those who nurture us and accept the important job of feeding, clothing, and disciplining us. The Scriptures teach us how important it is to train children in the difference between right and wrong—to raise up children who understand that people are for loving and that life is for learning. The most important lesson to learn is that—even though we may seem different on the outside—all of us are important in God's eyes. We are all part of the family of God. We are called to love whoever falls into our nest.

PRAYER:
Dear God, On Mother's Day we remember and bless those who care for us even when it isn't easy. Thank you for all mothers and for those who stand in for absent mothers, for their love reminds us of your love for us. Amen.

14
Assured of God's Presence: Ascension Day
The Kissing Hand

PASSAGE: Luke 24:50–53

PURPOSE: Although Jesus no longer walks the earth in the flesh, Christians are assured that Christ's love is always near.

PREPARATION: Children's Book
The Kissing Hand. Audrey Penn; Illustrations by Ruth E. Harper and Nancy M. Leak. Washington, DC: Child Welfare League of America, 1993.

Book Summary: When Chester the raccoon is reluctant to go to kindergarten for the first time, his mother teaches him a secret way to carry her love with him.

TEACHING TOOL: Sign language for "I Love You"

PRESENTATION:
Do any of you know American Sign Language? Maybe you know a little? I'd guess that all of you have seen this sign. (*Hold up one hand expressing the "I love you" sign.*) Do you know what this means? (*Allow volunteers to interpret or guess.*) This is one sign that means an entire phrase. The raised little finger on the hand stands for "I," meaning "me." The index and thumb form the sign for "L," which stands for "love." And the pinkie and pointer finger form the letter "Y," which stands for y-o-u! So what is the phrase? (*Say together, "I love you!"*) Yes! What a wonderful sign to share with others! I love

you! We all need to know that we are loved. Knowing someone loves us helps us to feel that we are not alone in the world. There's a wonderful children's book about the importance of knowing we are loved. It's called *The Kissing Hand* by Audrey Penn.

The story is about a little raccoon named Chester who is scared to leave his mother and his home to venture off to his first night at school. His mother, however, teaches him a secret sign that her mother had taught her. She has Chester open his hand, and right in the middle, she plants a loving kiss. This hand, she tells Chester, is his "kissing hand." Whenever he feels frightened or alone, he can press that hand to his cheek, and the warmth of the love she placed in that kiss will help him remember "Mommy loves you," and will fill him with toasty warm thoughts. The love, she assures him, won't wash off his kissing hand. Chester is able to go on to school and face life on his own because he has his "kissing hand" to remind him that he is not alone.

As Christians we have a story that helps us know that we are not alone, just like Chester's kissing hand story helped him. Forty days after his resurrection, Jesus gathered his disciples one last time just outside Jerusalem. Lifting up his hands, he blessed them; and as they watched, he was taken up into heaven, or we say he "ascended" to be with God. The disciples never forgot this moment. They passed the memory on to others who wrote the story down so that we could know that Jesus left us his blessing and so that we can remember that Jesus is now in heaven with God, watching over us. When Chester received the kissing hand from his mother, his response was to kiss his mother's hand in the same way so that she could know she was loved. When we think about Jesus raising his hand to bless his disciples, we might envision Jesus saying, "I love you." (*Hold up the hand sign.*) As we pray, perhaps we might want to return the same love we receive. (*Encourage everyone to make the "I love you" sign as they pray.*)

PRAYER:
Dear God, thank you for sending Jesus to show us how much we are loved. We just want to say, "We love you, too." Amen.

15
Strengthened by Memories:
Memorial Day
The Memory String

PASSAGE: Joshua 4:1–7

PURPOSE: Memories help us remember the past as we live in the present and look forward to the future.

PREPARATION: Children's Book
The Memory String. Eve Bunting; Pictures by Ted Rand. New York: Clarion Books, 2000.

Book Summary: While still grieving for her mother and unable to accept her stepmother, a girl clings to the memories represented by forty-three buttons on a string.

TEACHING TOOL: Buttons on a String

PRESENTATION:

Have you ever played with old buttons? (*Hold up the string of buttons and, if appropriate, relate a few personal memories associated with them.*) Buttons can serve as keepsakes to remind us of a particular person or event. Collecting some object as a reminder of important memories is even found in Bible stories. In the book of Joshua, the Scriptures record that God had Joshua collect twelve stones to represent the twelve tribes of Israel. Joshua then had men place the twelve stones in the Jordan River at the place where the waters had parted to let the Israelites cross safely with the Ark of the Covenant. The rocks were to be a memorial so that future generations could ask, "What happened here?" We human beings need ways to trigger our memories so important stories are not lost.

In a story by Eve Bunting called *The Memory String*, a little girl named Laura has forty-three buttons on a string that she inherited when her mother died. Laura treasures the family story behind each button that her mother had told her many times over the years. She likes to repeat the stories aloud to her cat, hoping that her stepmother will hear how much Laura still loves and remembers her mother. Maybe Laura was afraid that her new stepmother wanted to take her mother's place. As Laura is holding her cat Whiskers—forcing him to listen again to each button's story—Whiskers leaps from her arms and breaks the string holding Laura's memory collection. Although her dad and stepmother help Laura look, they can't find one button, the one from her father's uniform that Laura's mother had treasured. Later, after Laura is in bed, Laura overhears her stepmother insist on looking again with flashlights because she understands Laura will not want a substitute button—just like she doesn't want a substitute mother. When she finds the lost button, Laura's stepmother places it on the porch for Laura to discover as though it was magically returned to her. Laura doesn't tell that she knows what really happened; however, the returned button helps the little girl recognize that her stepmother understands and loves her. Laura also recognizes that she can continue adding to her string of memories. Maybe next she'll add a button belonging to her stepmother.

Laura's story told in *The Memory String* can help us understand the importance of celebrations like Memorial Day. Memorial Day began as a time to honor those soldiers who had died during the Civil War. Today we honor not only war veterans but also all those whose memories are important to us. Sometimes people take flowers or wreaths and place them on the headstones that mark the graves of family or friends who have died. Like Laura, we want to remember the stories of those we love, and then go on to make more memories for life.

PRAYER:
Dear God, thank you for times to remember the past and the people who have lived and died before us. Help us to honor their memories and your sustaining love. Amen.

16
Blessed by Diversity: Pentecost
People

Passage: Acts 2:1–14, 38–42

Purpose: The God who created the universe and all the people who dwell in it sends gifts through the Holy Spirit so that, though many, human beings are united in praise of God's goodness.

Preparation: Children's Book
People. Written and Illustrated by Peter Spier. Garden City, New York: Doubleday, 1980.

Book Summary: Through detailed illustrations, *People* celebrates the amazing differences among the billions of human beings on earth.

Teaching Tool: Kaleidoscope

Presentation:
I wonder why people are so fascinated with a kaleidoscope? *(Hold up a kaleidoscope and look through it.)* Do you like to look through a kaleidoscope? *(Pause to allow responses.)* I enjoy the beautiful shapes and colors, too. Isn't it amazing to see all the different combinations. No two patterns are exactly alike. Each one is beautiful in its own

way. That reminds me of a book called *People*, written and illustrated by Peter Spier. It's a story that is about a kaleidoscope of people.

Each of Spier's illustrations points out how unique people are. Although we all share the same general qualities—we have eyes, ears, and noses; we eat; we celebrate holidays; and we love to play games—the reality is that we all look different from each other. And, all the holidays and games we love are different depending upon what we choose to believe and where in the world we live. In the book, Peter Spier points out that sometimes people don't get along because they are different from each other. He says—and I believe he's right—that sometimes people hate each other because the "other" person looks different, acts differently, or believes differently. How do you think God feels about people hating each other for being different? Do you think God would say, "It's okay to hate others because they are different? I want everyone to be just like you!" *(Pause to reflect or guide responses.)* I don't think so!

In fact, in the church we have a special day called Pentecost that teaches us to celebrate diversity, or being different. On Pentecost, the Bible says, God's Holy Spirit visited the disciples in a special way. The rush of a mighty wind blew the timid disciples right out of their upper room and into the middle of a very diverse crowd of people. In fact, the Spirit gave these people from many different lands who spoke many different languages the ability to understand the message of the love of God made known to them in Jesus. The message of Pentecost is that God loves variety and sends a variety of gifts to all different kinds of people so that God's presence can be known everywhere there are people. In his book Peter Spier asks, "Wouldn't it be boring if we were all just alike?" I think that is an easy question to answer! Yes! God loves variety. God created and loves us all. Those of us who have experienced God's Holy Spirit are witnesses to God's great creative power available to everyone—no matter where we come from, what we look like, or what language we speak. The kaleidoscope can help us remember that God created people in infinite variety, just like the patterns we see inside the cylinder. But we can only appreciate the beautiful patterns in the kaleidoscope if we turn it toward the light. In the same way, if we look at people through the light of God's

Spirit, we will appreciate the grandeur of God's plan and celebrate the infinite gift of God's presence in the world around us.

PRAYER:
Dear God, give us eyes to see the beauty of your world in all its variety. Help us to view other people in the light of your love. Amen.

17
Revealed as One: Trinity Sunday
3 in 1 (A Picture of God)

PASSAGE: 2 Corinthians 13:13

PURPOSE: We can begin to understand the essence of God by recognizing the simple trinities found in nature.

PREPARATION: Children's Book
3 in 1 (A Picture of God). Joanne Marxhausen; Art by Benjamin Marxhausen. St. Louis, MO: Concordia Publishing House, 1973.

Book Summary: In *3 in 1 (A Picture of God)* Joanne Marxhausen explains the nature of God by examining an apple. Just as an apple is divided into three parts of peel, flesh, and core, so God is known as Father or Creator, Son or Savior, and Holy Spirit or Ever-present Power. Just as an apple has three parts yet is just one apple, so God can be known in three functions and yet be one God.

TEACHING TOOLS: Apple, paring knife

PRESENTATION:

How many apples do you see? (*Wait for someone to suggest "one."*) Yes, we can all easily tell that this is just one apple, correct? However, an apple has more than one part. What do we call this outer red covering on the apple? (*The peeling.*) This is the peeling. (*Cut the apple in half.*) If I cut the apple in half, we can see inside the apple. Here we find the part we love to eat, the flesh of the apple. It's different from the peeling, but they're both part of the apple, right? Now, inside the middle of the apple is the part that contains the seeds. Does anyone know what we call that part? (*The core.*) Yes, that's the apple core. So an apple is divided into three parts: The outer peel, the edible flesh, and the inner core that contains the seeds. How many apples then? Three? No! One apple, three parts!

That is exactly the message in a book called *3 in 1 (A Picture of God).* Joanne Marxhausen, who wrote the story, uses this understanding about apples to help children—and adults, too—understand something called "The Trinity." Do you know what we mean in the church when we talk about "The Trinity"? (*Let volunteers explain if possible.*) The book suggests that understanding God as a trinity is like understanding that peel, flesh, and core are still one apple. You see, we understand God as Father or Creator, the One who made us and protects us—just like the peeling shapes the appearance of the apple and protects the flesh from dangers of sun and insects. We also understand God as Jesus, the Son or Savior who came to earth to live and die for us. He was God in the flesh to show us how to live as a child of God, and he offered himself as a sacrifice for human error and sin. Finally, we understand God as Holy Spirit, the active power of God in creation. The Holy Spirit is given to believers as an indwelling presence helping us to be creative agents for God, just as the seeds in the apple's core bring to life more apple trees and apples. Although we have three ways of knowing about God, how many Gods do we have? Only one! Right! Just like there is only one apple.

When we hear ideas like *3 in 1,* we can sometimes feel confused and have trouble understanding concepts like God as a trinity. Isn't it just like our loving God to provide us with examples in nature that can help us understand the nature of God?! If we look around, we may discover lots of ways to think in three's—like the three leaves of the shamrock, or water that is also ice and steam, or even me who is a daughter, mother, and aunt (*or son, father, and uncle*). But those are other stories. Right now we're just thankful for apples. (*Cut up the apple and share slices with the participants.*)

PRAYER:
Dear God, thank you for making yourself known to us in three ways. Help us to look around and see all the ways nature has to show us your loving presence. Amen.

18

Answered in Love:
Father's Day
Does God Know How to Tie Shoes?

PASSAGE: Psalm 103:13

PURPOSE: Father's Day helps us to honor the One who has loved and protected us as children of God and who answers all our questions in life—just like a loving father.

PREPARATION: Children's Book
Does God Know How to Tie Shoes? Nancy White Carlstrom; Illustrated by Lori McElrath-Eslick. Grand Rapids, MI: William B. Eerdmans Publishing Company, 1993.

Book Summary: As Katrina is spending the day in the countryside, she asks her parents many questions about God. Her father and mother respond with ideas from Scripture, and Katrina adds her childlike wisdom about God's ever-present care.

TEACHING TOOL: Shoes with laces

PRESENTATION:
Do all of you know how to tie your shoes? *(Hold up a pair of shoes with laces.)* Good for you. Is anyone still learning? *(Acknowledge responses.)* Maybe your father helped or is helping you learn. At first it seems really impossible doesn't it? I remember when I was learning to tie my shoes. I would watch my father tie his shoes, and it seemed

like magic how fast he could do it. I started out like this: making two bunny ears and then tying them together. (*Demonstrate on the shoes.*) But my father could do it like this. (*Demonstrate the "hard" way, starting with just one loop and pulling the other around and through.*) I thought that was amazing. I thought my dad was amazing, too. Soon we will celebrate Father's Day and that's a good time to tell our dads how amazing we think they are.

Celebrating Father's Day is also a good time to remember that one of the ways we understand God is as a loving parent. In her book, *Does God Know How to Tie Shoes?*, Nancy White Carlstrom explores who God is in the voice of a young girl named Katrina talking with her parents. Katrina wonders aloud about God's abilities, and she thinks of God as she might think of a loving father. What kind of clothes does God wear? Does God like to paint? Can God tie his shoes? Katrina's parents don't make fun of her for asking silly questions about God. We know that God is not a man or a woman for that matter. God is Spirit. We know that God doesn't wear clothes or actually paint with a brush or keep pets. Yet God loves us just as we are, just as Katrina's parents love her. So they do not make fun of her questions, but instead offer her beautiful words from the Bible that help her to understand that God made the heavens and the earth. They explain that God doesn't have wings, yet God's love surrounds all of us like a mother hen protects her baby chicks. They even help her to understand that God must cry to see those who hurt or suffer or to see how people often treat each other. Most importantly, Katrina's parents help her to understand that she can talk to God simply—just like she talks to her daddy.

On Father's Day we want to remember and honor those who are our fathers or who have been like fathers to us in life—whether they taught us how to tie our shoes or how to talk to God.

PRAYER:
Dear God, thank you for our fathers and grandfathers and for those who father and protect us in many ways. Help us to understand that you love us like that, too. Amen.

19

United as One: Fourth of July
Stone Soup

PASSAGE: John 17:22–23

PURPOSE: On the Fourth of July, we celebrate the unity that comes when diverse gifts are offered for the common good.

PREPARATION: Children's Book
Stone Soup: An Old Tale. Told and pictured by Marcia Brown. New York: Scribner, 1947.

Summary: Soldiers making their way home pass through a village and ask the townspeople for something to eat and a place to sleep. Distrusting and fearful, the peasants refuse, claiming a lack of food or room for the men. Thinking on their feet, the soldiers announce their plan to make stone soup. Intrigued, the astonished townspeople aid the men in their task, providing them with a huge soup cauldron, water, and whatever ingredients the soldiers casually mention. By the end of the evening everyone sits down to a hearty meal to which each has made a contribution.

TEACHING TOOLS: Soup pot, stone

PRESENTATION:
Does anyone know the recipe for stone soup? I think that I have the main ingredients. (*Hold up the soup pot and one stone.*) Has anyone ever eaten stone soup? I understand it is very good! (*Wait to see if*

anyone volunteers a response.) If you have never eaten stone soup, then you probably don't know the story either. Actually, the story itself is an old French tale told and retold for generations. However, in 1947, Marcia Brown wrote down the tale so that many people could appreciate the story's wisdom and learn the recipe.

In Marcia Brown's illustrated book, *Stone Soup*, soldiers are tired and hungry as they pass through a small village. They ask the villagers for food and a place to sleep. However, the people in the village are fearful and say they are poor and don't have food or room enough to share. Instead of being angry, the soldiers shrug off the townspeople's selfishness and suggest—so that the people overhear—that they will simply make "stone soup." They only need someone to loan them a pot. Curious, one person offers them a pot for the stone the soldiers provide. As they add water and build a fire, the soldiers taste their "stone soup" and comment that just one more ingredient would add so much to the flavor. Soon the curious onlookers offer to share the one ingredient he or she can contribute, like a carrot, a potato, a turnip, beans, or celery. By the time each one has provided a vegetable to add to the broth, guess what!—the empty pot is brimming full of a wonderful collection of flavors, and everyone in the village enjoys a bowl of "stone soup." They all enjoy the experience so much, the townsfolk end up offering the soldiers the best beds in the village for their night's rest. And all of this sharing came from one stone and an empty pot!

The story of "stone soup" is a good way to think about the Fourth of July holiday we share as a nation. If we are to continue to prosper and celebrate our freedom, then each individual American must share his or her idea, talent, or ability for the good of all. If we each give something of ourselves to our nation's "pot" (*hold up the soup pot*), we will all be nourished and have what we need for life. Just like the recipe for "stone soup," the recipe for a democracy requires people to pool their wisdom, their energy, and their money so that everyone has the opportunity to prosper and to enjoy individual freedom. While the Fourth of July is a national holiday, those of us in the church believe that freedom and democracy represent God's idea of what's best for people. Before Jesus left the earth, he prayed for his disciples to become one. Jesus didn't pray for us to become the same; instead, he prayed for his followers to be united with God, just as he was. If all of God's creation, as different as we are, give our lives to God's use, guess what we become? A zesty and flavorful concoction that God can use to bless the entire world—just like a pot of "stone soup"! What a recipe!

PRAYER:
Dear God, thank you for providing each of us with something to share with others. Help us to unselfishly contribute so that we may all be blessed. Amen.

20
Honored as Important: Labor Day
You Are Special

PASSAGE: Psalm 90:17

PURPOSE: While work establishes the pattern for our lives, God establishes our worth.

PREPARATION: Children's Book
You Are Special. Max Lucado; Illustrations by Sergio Martinez. Wheaton, IL: Crossway Books, 1997.

Book Summary: Punchinello receives only dots for his faults from the other Wemmicks until he visits his creator and learns his true worth.

TEACHING TOOL: Star stickers

PRESENTATION:
Have you ever gotten a paper with a star on it? (*Hold up the star stickers.*) What does that mean? (*Allow someone to explain that a star means "well done."*) We usually feel really good when someone judges our work to be worthy of a star, right? It is almost like they put the star on us instead of on the paper! What happens when our work isn't as good as it could be? (*Let the participants suggest what poor work receives: a zero, a "do over" stamp, or other mark.*) How do we feel when we get a mark that says our work doesn't measure up? Does it seem that we might as well wear that mark on our foreheads? Unfortunately, sometimes we human beings confuse the work we do

with who we are. As we get ready to celebrate Labor Day, maybe we should hear about a story that helps us sort out "being" and "doing."

In the story *You Are Special* by Max Lucado, the Wemmicks were wooden people who were all made by a woodworker named Eli. Every day the Wemmicks went around placing stickers on one another. On those who had talent or did special things, they placed stars. On those whose paint was chipped or who were clumsy, they placed dots. One Wemmick named Punchinello always received dots. No matter how hard he tried, he always seemed to fall or do something silly. Pretty soon people were giving him dots for no reason at all. Pretty soon Punchinello began to believe that he only deserved dots, and he only hung around other people who had dots. Then one day Punchinello met a girl named Lucia who didn't have any dots or any stars. Others would try to place stickers on her, but they simply fell off. Punchinello thought he would like to be like that, so he asked her how she did it. "It's easy," Lucia replied. "Every day I go see Eli, the Woodcarver." Punchinello followed Lucia's advice, even though he wasn't sure that Eli would want to see him. Punchinello discovered that Eli knew him by name because Eli had made Punchinello in the first place. Eli told him the secret to keep the stars and dots from sticking. Punchinello had to believe that it was only Eli's opinion of him that mattered—and Eli believed Punchinello was pretty special. As Punchinello left Eli's workshop, Eli reminded him to visit every day so that the little Wemmick could remember how much Eli believed in him. "I think he really means it!" thought Punchinello— and the first dot fell off!

Of course, Max Lucado wants us to think of ourselves as Punchinello and of God as Eli. No matter how much we try to be perfect, no one is good at everything. No matter how important a job we find, or how much money we make, no amount of human praise can make us worthwhile. Only God can help us know our true value. That doesn't mean doing good work isn't important. The Psalmist prays in Psalm 90 for God to "establish the work of our hands." God gives each of us talents and abilities that we can use and develop in order to do good work in the world. What is important, however, is that we recognize that each of us is unique and important to God, no matter what we do for a living, or how many stars—or dots—the world wants to stick on us. As we rest from our labors on Labor Day and celebrate all the different workers it takes to make our nation great, we can also celebrate that each of us is a work of God. It is who we are, not what we do, that matters most!

PRAYER:

Dear God, thank you for giving us meaningful work to do in the world. Help us to work at seeing each other and ourselves as your valuable creations. Amen.

21

Invited to Share:
World Communion Sunday
Potluck

PASSAGE: Psalm 34:8

PURPOSE: At God's feast there is room for all to share and enjoy.

PREPARATION: Children's Book
Potluck. Anne Shelby; Pictures by Irene Trivas. New York: Orchard Books, 1991.

Book Summary: Alpha and Betty have a potluck and all their friends—from Acton to Zelda—bring appropriate alphabetical food ranging from asparagus soup to zucchini casserole.

TEACHING TOOL: Breadbasket

PRESENTATION:
How many of you have ever been to a potluck? *(Wait for a show of hands and ask a volunteer to explain what "potluck" means.)* When we go to a potluck, we often bring a dish that's a specialty we love to make. What specialty might you expect to find in a basket like this one? *(Hold up the breadbasket.)* I suppose it could hold lots of things, but I use this as a breadbasket. Yum! There's nothing better than homemade bread!

Do you think that you could come up with at least twenty-six kinds of food you might find at a potluck? Suppose I asked you to come up with twenty-six foods that each started with a different letter of the alphabet. Wow! That would make it even harder, right? In her book *Potluck*, Anne Shelby does exactly that. In her story, two friends plan a potluck party—Alpha and Betty—get it? Alpha and Betty—alphabet! When Alpha and Betty invite their thirty-one friends, from Acton to Zeke and Zelda, each is instructed to bring a food that starts with the first letter of his or her name. What do you suppose Acton might bring? *(Pause to let the group brainstorm "A" foods if time permits.)* Actually, Acton brings asparagus soup and Zelda brings zucchini casserole! Can you imagine what a feast their friends create when each one brings something different? Wow! Amazing!

In the church, we have a similar kind of meal—not exactly a potluck. But everyone is invited to this meal—in fact we invite all of the Christians around the world! And the food represents the Alpha and the Omega, the A and the Z from the Greek alphabet, which is another name for Christ. The meal that I mean occurs on World Communion Sunday. On that agreed upon Sunday, Christians around the world observe the sacrament. They take communion in order to share God's feast of love in a way that celebrates our close relationship to one another no matter where we live, no matter what color our skin might be, and no matter whether our church is rich or poor, large or small. On that one day we emphasize that we are one family in God's name all around the world as we share the bread and cup that Jesus said would represent his body and his blood. Now, Alpha and Betty had a wonderful time with all of their friends in their A to Z potluck. But I think God's potluck is a celebration that is even more amazing!

PRAYER:
Dear God, thank you for being the beginning and the end, the A to Z of life. Help us to invite everyone to share in your feast of love. Amen.

22

Shaped for Service:
Reformation Day
Swimmy

PASSAGE: Romans 12:2

PURPOSE: God's church is ever open to God's leading Spirit, to be transformed and renewed from within.

PREPARATION: Children's Book
Swimmy. Leo Lionni. New York: Pantheon, 1963.

Book Summary: In this classic story, Swimmy, a small orphaned fish, shows his friends how—with ingenuity, and hard work—they can conquer their fears and overcome the dangers of the wet world.

TEACHING TOOL: Inflatable fish

PRESENTATION:

Something is wrong with my fish. He's rather flat. I wonder what he needs? *(Allow respondents to make suggestions.)* Oh, I see, there's a place here to blow in some air so my fish will take shape. *(If possible, inflate the fish.)* Without air inside, the fish didn't look like it was supposed to, did it? Maybe this fish never went to school! Did you know that small fish in the ocean swim in schools? That doesn't mean that they learn to read, but it does mean that they swim together and help one another. In fact, there is a story called *Swimmy* about a little fish that loses his family and for awhile is all alone in the big wet world of the ocean. That would be scary, right?

Swimmy is really quite brave. Even though he is traveling alone through the ocean, he enjoys seeing all the different forms of life, like the jellyfish and lobsters that look interesting to Swimmy. Fortunately for Swimmy, he finds another group of fish just like himself. They are hiding at the bottom of a large rock and are afraid to come see the sights with Swimmy because they know that bigger fish could eat them. Inspired, Swimmy suggests that they swim together in formation so that they look like the biggest fish in the sea. Together they form a very large presence with Swimmy serving as the "eye" of their big-fish shape. Now they can swim through the ocean without fear of being eaten. Swimmy was a really smart little fish!

The story of Swimmy is a good story for the church today. Sometimes Christians have tried to go through life alone. Like Swimmy, we recognize we are better off to share the life of faith with others. Even when we join forces as a church, sometimes the group seems to be hiding rather than living boldly in the world God sent Jesus to save. Like the fish in the story, we must learn to work together to be the image of Christ. When we let God's Spirit re-form us in the image of Christ, we can accomplish much more. On this Reformation Sunday, we celebrate that God shaped the church and continues to re-shape us or "reform" us so that we are filled with the Spirit and are about the work that God assigns us to do. We just have to be filled with the Spirit and stay in formation! (*Hold up the inflated fish.*)

Prayer:
Dear God, thank you for providing a church for us to find strength and renewal. Help our church to live boldly as your people in this place. Amen.

23
Remembered by Heart: All Saints' Day
Granddad's Prayers of the Earth

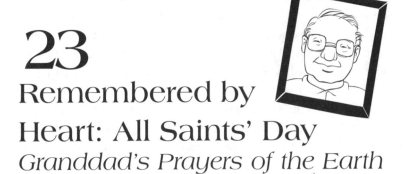

Passage: Hebrews 12:1

Purpose: When we see with eyes of faith and hear with a heart of love, then we can sense the presence of all those who have gone before us and who live now in God's eternal embrace.

Preparation: Children's Book
Granddad's Prayers of the Earth. Douglas Wood; Illustrated by P. J. Lynch. Cambridge, MA: Candlewick Press, 1999.

Book Summary: Because his granddad has explained how all things in the natural world pray and contribute to the beauty of life, a grandson finds comfort after his granddad dies.

Teaching Tool: Picture of deceased grandfather or great-grandfather

---

Presentation:
I'd like to introduce you to someone. (*Hold up a picture and briefly relate the name and the relationship of the person in the photo.*) I'm sure that each of you has pictures of family members who are no longer living on earth. On All Saints' Day, we remember the people who have gone before us, especially those who have left us a legacy of faith. Sometimes we only know stories about them that our family has passed down; often we read Biblical accounts about the saints whose lives and deeds are recorded in the Scriptures. Sometimes we

are fortunate enough for our saints in the faith to still be alive while we are young, and we learn from them directly about faith and life.

Douglas Wood was one boy who was fortunate enough to experience his grandad's wisdom as he was growing up. Later in life, he wrote a book called *Granddad's Prayers of the Earth* so that he could share with others what he had learned. Like other little boys, Douglas asked his grandad lots of "what if" and "why is it" questions. One day he asked his grandad about prayer. Rather than teaching him words to say or talking about God in ways that a little boy could never understand, Douglas's grandad simply used the beauties of nature to demonstrate prayer. His granddad's answer was that all of creation is a prayer. The trees reach for heaven; the rocks wait, still and silent. Water can pray by being silent and deep, or by laughing and dancing. The tall grass waves its arms in prayer; the flowers breathe out the sweetness of their prayers into the air. The wind whispers and moans, praying and singing a hymn at the same time. Douglas's grandad explained that people pray wonderful prayers, too. Some prayers are as simple as bending down to smell a flower or watching the sunrise. Making music or painting a picture can be a human's prayer as well. Douglas wondered if prayers were answered, but his grandad explained that most prayers weren't questions. He taught Douglas that we pray because we are here, not to change the world, but to change ourselves. Yet when we change ourselves, the world does change. Although Douglas believed his grandad, he didn't really understand everything he was taught about prayer until his grandad died. Then, in his grief, as he sat on a rock and listened to the breeze, he began to hear the prayers his granddad had explained to him. As he was able to join in thanksgiving for his grandad's life, Douglas felt something change within himself. And, he knew his grandad was near.

All Saints' Day teaches us to recognize there is a world we cannot see with human eyes. In the book of Hebrews in the Bible, the writer says we are surrounded by a great cloud of witnesses. Those witnesses are the people of faith who have come before us. As we learn to quiet our hearts, we can sense a change in ourselves, too. Like Douglas, we can know that love connects us to eternity, where all of us live in the presence of God.

PRAYER:

Dear God, thank you for the loving examples of the saints who have come before us. Help us to live with confidence each day and leave behind us a legacy of hope for those who follow. Amen.

24

Remembered with Gratitude: Thanksgiving Day
Something from Nothing

PASSAGE: 1 Thessalonians 5:18

PURPOSE: If our hearts are grateful, we can make something from nothing.

PREPARATION: Children's Book
Something from Nothing. Adapted from a Jewish folktale by Phoebe Gilman. New York: Scholastic, 1992.

Book Summary: *Something from Nothing* is a retelling of a Jewish folktale. Joseph's baby blanket is transformed into ever smaller items as he grows until nothing is left—but then Joseph gets an idea.

TEACHING TOOL: Baby blanket

PRESENTATION:
Did any of you have a special blanket that you loved when you were small? I would guess that you did! Even if you don't remember it anymore, you probably once had a blanket or a quilt that was a great comfort to you when you lay down to sleep. (*Hold up a baby blanket and, if possible, briefly relate the family story behind it.*) I would expect that most of your parents could tell a story about a blanket that you loved when you were little. That kind of memory is what is behind the children's book called *Something from Nothing*.

The story Phoebe Gilman tells is a traditional Jewish folk tale, but it is an account that every person and every culture can appreciate. A little boy named Joseph has a favorite blanket. As it becomes old and frayed around the edges, his mother tells him that he must get rid of it. Instead, Joseph's grandfather turns it into a little jacket for Joseph to wear. But when the jacket becomes old and shabby, again his mother tells him to throw it out. Instead, Joseph's grandfather cuts it down to make a vest. You can guess what happens! The vest gets old and worn, and Joseph's mother tells him to "Throw it out!" But stubbornly, Joseph takes it to grandfather who transforms the remaining good parts into a tie for Joseph to wear. Finally, the old, spotted tie becomes a covered button for Joseph's pants. That's all he has left of his precious blanket. But then, something terrible happens! The button pops off of Joseph's pants! Oh, no! Joseph's mother said, "Even grandfather can't make something from nothing." But Joseph discovers there is still something that remains. So he took paper and pen and—wrote the story!

Something from Nothing is a great story any time of the year, but it is an especially good one to read at Thanksgiving Day. Sometimes people throw away clothes, furniture, blankets—even relationships when they are old and worn. *Something from Nothing* teaches us to value the blessings from the past by recycling what we have to make the most of our possessions. When we live in a throwaway society, we only seem to appreciate what is new. The message of Thanksgiving is to be grateful for what we have, not to be so quick just to throw away what is older or outgrown. However, the most important message of this story is that—even when we must get rid of or even when we lose those things that have been important to us, we still have a reason to be thankful—because we have the memory, and memories can be shared. If you think about it, the ungrateful heart looks at life and sees nothing; but the grateful heart can make something even from nothing!

PRAYER:
Dear God, thank you for all the good things that you provide in our lives. Help us to savor them, recycle them, and at least remember them in your honor. Amen.

25

Named by All:
Reign of Christ Sunday
In God's Name

PASSAGE: Psalm 135:13

PURPOSE: As we search through many names for God, we begin to glimpse God's majesty.

PREPARATION: Children's Book
In God's Name. Sandy Eisenberg Sasso; Illustrated by Phoebe Stone. Woodstock, VT: Jewish Lights Publishing, 1994.

Book Summary: After the creation of the world no one knows the name for God. So each person searches, and each seeker claims that he or she alone knows the answer. Finally, all come together and learn what God's name really is.

TEACHING TOOL: Mirror

PRESENTATION:
Whose face do you see in this mirror? (*Hand the mirror to a volunteer who should see his or her own face.*) No, that can't be right. Give the mirror to someone else. Who do you see in the mirror? (*Repeat the sequence several times, as appropriate.*) No! You are all confused. Give me the mirror. See! I'm the face in the mirror! Why do you keep telling me you see someone different? (*Let volunteers try to explain.*) Okay, I understand now. Because a mirror reflects light from the image before it, we see our own faces as we look at the polished surface. Of course, now it makes sense. We are all right! I think the mirror can

help us understand this special day in the life of the church. This is "Reign of Christ" Sunday, the last day of the church year. Today we celebrate that Christ is the Messiah, the one who reigns over the entire world. When we use the name "King" in a way to understand God, sometimes people get the wrong impression. Maybe a book I know will help us sort out how we use different names for God.

The book I am thinking of is called *In God's Name* by Sandy Eisenberg Sasso. The story starts at the beginning of the world when all the plants and animals and people received a name. But no one knew God's name. So everyone began to search for a name for God. A farmer whose skin was dark as the soil he tilled called God "Source of Life." The one who tended sheep in the valley called God "Shepherd." An artist who carved figures from stone called God "My Rock." The young man holding his baby daughter called God "Father." A young woman nursing her baby son called God "Mother." Each one thought that his or her name for God was best. People argued over who knew the right name for God, and each called everyone else's names "wrong." But no one listened, least of all God. Finally, all the different people came together and knelt by a pool of water with a surface as shiny as a mirror. At the same time that they called out their names for God, they looked into the mirrored surface of the water. Suddenly, they understood that all of their names for God were good. And they understood that God's name was "One."

On Reign of Christ Sunday, we celebrate that for Christians Jesus is the head of the Church, the Anointed One of God, our King. Christ has won the victory over death and reigns in heaven with God Almighty. But "king" is only one name for our understanding of God in Christ. Like a king, Christ is triumphant and powerful. But Christ is also our friend, our shepherd. Jesus told us he is like a mother hen that gathers us under her wings and is our protector. So on this last day of the church year we celebrate all the ways we have come to know God as our Creator, as our Savior, and as our Helper: three understandings of God, but only one God. As God's children, we understand that all our names for God help us learn more about who God is and how we can be more like God in our everyday lives. Maybe, like the characters in our story, we can come to see God mirrored in the faces of everyone we meet, and we can learn that God's name truly is "One."

PRAYER:

Dear God, thank you for all the ways you make yourself known to us. Help us to understand that you are the One force we see reflected in so many ways. Amen.

26

Revealed for the World:
First Sunday in Advent
Snowflake Bentley

PASSAGE: Isaiah 55:10, 11

PURPOSE: In Advent we remember that God sent Jesus in the form of a person to affirm God's love and to secure each believer's salvation.

PREPARATION: Children's Book
Snowflake Bentley. Jacqueline Briggs Martin; Illustrated by Mary Azarian. Boston: Houghton Mifflin, 1998.

Book Summary: *Snowflake Bentley* is a biography of a self-taught scientist who photographed thousands of individual snowflakes in order to study their unique formations.

TEACHING TOOL: Snowflake

PRESENTATION:
It's time to start thinking about Christmas! Yes, today is the first Sunday in Advent, a season of getting ready for Jesus to be re-born in our hearts. Have any of you ever made decorations that look like this? (*Hold up a cut paper snowflake.*) Why do we think of snow-flakes at Christmas? (*Pause for possible explanations.*) It can snow in Bethlehem, but we don't know that there was snow when Jesus was born. Maybe we think of a "white Christmas" because snow seems like a magic blanket that unites everything and makes the world

seem clean and new. I know the story of a man who loved snow so much that he spent his whole life trying to take pictures of snowflakes.

His name was Wilson Bentley and he grew up in Vermont in the late 1800s. Vermont is a place where a lot of snow falls, so it was good that Willie loved the snow! As a young boy, Willie tried to catch snowflakes and study them. He attempted to draw their pictures, but the flakes would melt before he could finish. Even though his parents thought this passion for snowflakes was silly, they bought their son a new invention called a magnifying camera so that he could enlarge and photograph a snowflake and study its design. Willie began what became a lifelong mission:to show the world the beauty he found in each individual snowflake. Willie had discovered that no two flakes were exactly alike—each one was a unique work of art. For more than fifty years, this simple farmer who had no special training in scientific study dedicated his life to revealing the mystery and beauty of the snowflake. Willie never became rich or famous because he always put the money he earned for his photographs into equipment and books. Yet even scientists recognized Willie's great accomplishments. People began to call him "Snowflake Bentley." After Willie died, children in his town worked to create a museum in his honor. Snowflake Bentley's mission was accomplished. He found a way to save snowflakes so that the world could love their beauty as he did.

As we get ready for Christmas, the *Snowflake Bentley* story reminds us of God's mission in sending Jesus to the world. Jesus came to show how much God loves each of us. Like snowflakes, each of us is unique and beautiful. Jesus came to save people from being lost in sin. Allowing Jesus to be reborn in our hearts saves us, just like Snowflake Bentley's photographs preserved each snowflake's beauty. Because of his love of snow, Willie became known as "Snowflake." When we begin to see the beauty in each person as God does, we then begin to understand what it means for our names to include the word "Christian."

PRAYER:
Dear God, thank you for sending Jesus to save us. Help us to see the beauty of each person with your eyes of love. Amen.

27
Humbled by Generosity:
Second Sunday in Advent
The Quiltmaker's Gift

Passage: 2 Corinthians 8:9

Purpose: As we think of Christ's generosity during Advent, we are humbled and made rich by giving to others in Christ's name.

Preparation: Children's Book
The Quiltmaker's Gift. by Jeff Brumbeau; Pictures by Gail de Marcken. Duluth, MN: Pfeifer-Hamilton, 2000.

Book Summary: When a generous quiltmaker finally agrees to make a quilt for a greedy king, but only under certain conditions, she causes him to undergo a change of heart.

Teaching Tool: Patchwork quilt

Presentation:
Do any of you have a family treasure like this at home? (*Show the patchwork quilt.*) In the past, quilts were the bedding for poor families because they sewed together scraps of cloth from old dresses and shirts to make a blanket. Then they would stuff cotton between the top pieces of cloth and an inexpensive backing material. Finally, they would sew by hand through the top and bottom layers to hold

the stuffing in place. That process is called "quilting." Today, when so many blankets can be made cheaply by machines, hand-sewn quilts are considered special works of art and can be very expensive to purchase. The best kinds of quilts are the ones that are gifts from people who have sewn each stitch with love. There is a story about a quiltmaker that can help us think about what is important during this season of gift giving and exchanging of "wish lists."

The book is called *The Quiltmaker's Gift* by Jeff Brumbeau and Gail de Marcken. In the story, an old woman is known all around the countryside for the beautiful quilts she makes. However, the quiltmaker will not sell her quilts. She only presents them as gifts to people who are poor and in need. A greedy king lives in the same country. He is so selfish that he decides to have two birthdays a year so that he can command more presents. Despite his orders for people everywhere to give him gifts, the king is not happy. When he hears of the beautiful quilts made by the old woman, he decides to demand that she give him one so that maybe he will finally be happy. When the king and his soldiers arrive to seize the king's present by force if necessary, the old woman, seeing the king's greed, tosses her quilt out the window because she only gives them to people in need. The king punishes the old woman for denying what he believes will make him happy, but she tells him she will only make a quilt for him if he gives away everything he owns. For each treasure he gives, she will sew one patch on the quilt. Finally, the king begins to part with his treasures. Gift by gift, the king discovers happiness by seeing the joy he brings to those with whom he shares. The king does receive his quilt, but he uses it for a cover on his wagon as he travels around the countryside giving away more of his possessions. And in exchange for the quiltmaker's gift, he offers her his throne as a comfortable place to do her sewing.

This story helps us understand the message of Christmas in an important way. Often, like the greedy king, we only think of Christmas in terms of what we get. However, that is not the meaning of Christmas. Jesus did not have to give up his place in heaven with God to accept the difficulties of life—to sacrifice his life on a cross for people who too often think only of themselves. Yet that is just what Jesus did for each of us. When we think of Christ's generosity in coming to earth, we have to consider what that means about our choices, especially at Christmas. Maybe we can learn something from the greedy king. If we really want to find happiness, we can discover it only as we learn to give what we possess to others—maybe "things" we own, but also our time, our energy, and—most importantly—our love.

PRAYER:
Dear God, thank you for the gift of Jesus at Christmas. Help us to respond to your love by sharing our gifts with others. Amen.

28
Shared in Joy:
Third Sunday in Advent
The Clown of God

PASSAGE: 2 Corinthians 9:15

PURPOSE: As Christmas draws nearer, we respond to God's gift by sharing our own gifts in joy.

PREPARATION: Children's Book
The Clown of God: An Old Story. Told and illustrated by Tomie dePaola. San Diego: Harcourt Brace Jovanovich, 1978.

Book Summary: A once famous Italian juggler, now old and a beggar, gives one final performance before a statue of Our Lady and the Holy Child with miraculous results.

TEACHING TOOL: Juggling balls

PRESENTATION:
Have any of you learned to juggle? *(Display the balls and attempt to juggle or invite a juggler to perform.)* Juggling looks so easy when you watch someone who knows how to do it! Some folks just seem to have a natural talent for juggling. It's a gift you might say. Others of us struggle to learn even to juggle just three little balls. What if someone could juggle lots of things, like plates and clubs and torches! That would be quite a juggling gift, I'd say. There is an old French legend about a juggler and the Christ Child that author Tomie dePaola retold and illustrated in the book *The Clown of God.*

In the legend, a young orphaned boy has a gift for juggling, and that is the way this poor child manages to earn his food to eat. He juggles fruit for a vendor to draw a crowd. The people applaud, buy produce from the merchant, and the seller's wife feeds the boy, named Giovanni, a bowl of soup for his performance. When a group of traveling players comes through his little village, Giovanni convinces them to let him join their troupe by offering to juggle. That begins Giovanni's life as a famous juggler. He becomes well-known and well-to-do, but he remembers what it is like to be poor and shares what he has with traveling beggars. However, Giovanni, like all human beings, grows old. He can no longer perform, and his talents are no longer appreciated. An old beggar now himself, he finds shelter in a church on the night of the "procession of the gifts" on Christmas Eve. He watches people parade to the statue of Mary and the Holy Child with all of their magnificent gifts. But what could Giovanni give? Inspired, Giovanni decides to present a final performance before the statue as his gift to the Christ Child. Giovanni juggles better than he ever has before! His finale was always the rainbow of balls, six colors with the final gold one as the "sun in the heavens." "For You, Sweet Child! For You!" he cries. With this triumphant offering, Giovanni collapses and dies. When the priest looks from Giovanni's body to the statue, the Christ Child is smiling and holding the golden ball.

This legend is somewhat sad and happy at the same time. Yet, we learn an important lesson to remember as the time for Christmas draws nearer. God has given each of us gifts, talents, and abilities to use and to share with God's world. God has given us an even greater gift, however. That is the gift of Jesus. How can we thank God for giving us so much? Like the old "Clown of God," we can find true joy by presenting our gifts back to God as an offering of praise and thanksgiving. What better gift to get for Christmas than the thought that we can make the Christ Child smile.

PRAYER:
Dear God, we know that you have given us each special gifts for life. Thank you. This Christmas, we offer them back to you with grateful hearts. Amen.

29
Crafted with Care:
Fourth Sunday in Advent
The Christmas Miracle of Jonathan Toomey

PASSAGE: 1 John 4:15

PURPOSE: God prepares us for Christmas by helping us make room in our hearts for others.

PREPARATION: Children's Book
The Christmas Miracle of Jonathan Toomey. Susan Wojciechowski; Illustrated by P. J. Lynch. Cambridge, MA: Candlewick Press, 1995.

Book Summary: The widow McDowell and her seven-year-old son Thomas ask the gruff Jonathan Toomey, the best wood-worker in the valley, to carve the figures of their Christmas creche.

TEACHING TOOL: Block of wood

PRESENTATION:

What do you see? (*Hold up a block of wood.*) You see a block of wood, right? What else can you see? Can you see a sheep, or a donkey, or a camel? How about a shepherd or an angel or the baby Jesus? No? I think if you could see with a woodcarver's eyes that you might be able to see those things. Michelangelo, the famous sculptor and artist, once said of a block of marble, "There is an angel trapped in there, and I am going to set him free." Something that makes an artist different is that he or she is able to see the possibilities in something the rest of us might miss. That's true of God, too. There is a story about a woodcarver that teaches us to remember, especially at Christmas, that God sees possibilities in people, just like artists see possibilities in wood or stone.

The book is called *The Christmas Miracle of Jonathan Toomey* by Susan Wojciechowski. This special Christmas story, set in the 1800s, is about a woodcarver named Jonathan Toomey whom everyone called Jonathan *Gloomy*. But Jonathan had a reason to be unhappy. He had lost his wife and baby within a few days of each other. He was so sad that he packed up everything and moved far away from his memories. However, Jonathan forgot that God crafted our hearts to turn toward others, not to close off and become hard like stone or a piece of wood. That's why everyone thought him so gloomy—he kept to himself and simply practiced his trade of woodcarving. That's the way he was making a living—without really living—until a new customer asked him to recreate a crèche, or nativity set, that she had lost when she moved. The widow McDowell and her young son, Thomas, came to watch on occasion, and grudgingly, Jonathan Toomey let young Thomas sit quietly and observe a master woodcarver at work. Over the weeks, the crèche animals began to take shape, but not without a few suggestions from his youthful colleague. Thomas lets Jonathan know that the sheep should look happy because they were with baby Jesus. The cow should look proud to warm the stable, and the angel should look important. Thomas's mother also brought Mr. Toomey baked goods and special gifts she had made for him even though he continued to be gruff and standoffish. Like Jonathan could look into the wood and see the scene from Bethlehem emerge, Thomas and his mother saw goodness in Mr. Toomey. When faced with carving the last two figures, Jonathan could not find inspiration until he took out a picture, long hidden away, of his wife and child. When he dried his tears, he spent Christmas Eve shaping the figures of Mary and Jesus. On Christmas morning, Toomey brought the completed nativity set to the McDowell's and went with them to church to celebrate the gift of the Christ Child. After that, no one called him Mr. Gloomy anymore.

The story shows quite a transformation! God's miraculous love changed Jonathan Toomey, with the help of widow McDowell and Thomas. They were able to see past the gruff exterior to the goodness that others had missed. Their gift of acceptance enabled Jonathan Toomey to find God's gift of love in the image of his wife and child. During Advent, we remember that God saw potential in us and sent Jesus to be our Savior. Perhaps, then, the best Christmas gift we can give is to see in one another the face of God.

PRAYER:

Dear God, thank you for sending Jesus to show us your love. Help us to bring out your best in each other. Amen.

30

Born to Give: Christmas
What Can I Give Him?

PASSAGE: Luke 2:1–7

PURPOSE: When we contemplate the gift of love received at Christmas, our hearts long to respond in kind.

PREPARATION: Children's Book
What Can I Give Him? Based on a Poem by Christina Georgina Rossetti. Debi Gliori. New York: Holiday House, 1998.

Book Summary: With the words of Christina Rossetti's poem as the text, illustrations depict two girls' stories at Christmas as each must choose a special gift for someone very important.

TEACHING TOOL: Heart ornament

PRESENTATION:

What can I do with my heart? (*Hold up the heart-shaped Christmas ornament.*) Well, this isn't my actual heart, of course. This is an ornament with a hook ready for hanging. Where do we usually place ornaments? (*Pause for response.*) Of course! Ornaments are meant for hanging on Christmas trees, right? When Jesus was born in Bethlehem, do you think that Mary and Joseph decorated a tree in the stable? (*Let the participants ponder the possibility.*) None of us was actually there, but I think we can safely assume that there were no decorated trees to celebrate Jesus' birth. The tradition of Christmas trees came along much later. And yet, what we do today to celebrate Christmas is meant to remind us of the actual events when Jesus was born long ago.

A writer named Debi Gliori created a beautiful picture book called *What Can I Give Him?* to help us do that. She took a poem by Christina Rossetti originally titled "A Christmas Carol" and illustrated those words with two pictures on each page. The first pictures portray a little girl as she shares a winter day with her grandpa as they walk, build a snowman, feed the birds, and read together by the fire. The second picture on each page takes us back to Bethlehem and a little girl who works in the stable where Jesus was born as she tends the animals, carries water, and observes Mary and Joseph with their new baby boy. *(If possible, read the poem and show the illustrations, allowing the participants to make the connections between the two "worlds.")* The modern girl longs to give her special grandfather a present, but she has no money, just like the poor little girl in the Bethlehem stable who watches the shepherds and wise men bring gifts to the Christ Child. To bless her grandfather, the little girl makes a picture of the sheep and the Wise Men from the Christmas story and gives it to him. Do you think her grandpa would like that gift? *(Guide responses to discuss that making gifts for someone is a gift from the heart.)* When we give something we've made, we're giving a part of ourselves, aren't we? In the book you have to look closely to see what the little girl in Bethlehem has given. *(If possible, point out the pictures.)* We see that she removes her coat. What might the baby Jesus do with her coat? *(Point to the Christmas card in the final picture.)* As we see Grandpa hug his granddaughter, we can also see on the mantle the Christmas card that shows baby Jesus, warm and happy, wrapped in the stable girl's coat.

The time when Jesus was born is different than the world we live in today in many ways. We've added new inventions—like Christmas trees. But, guess what? The very best gift we can give each other is still the same. As the poem says, "What can I give him? Give my heart."

PRAYER:
Dear God, thank you for giving us Jesus to bring your love to earth. Help us to pass along Christ's gift of love to everyone we meet. Amen.

Bibliography
Children's
Picture Books

3 in 1 (A Picture of God). Marxhausen, Joanne and Benjamin Marxhausen, Illustrator. St. Louis, MO: Concordia Publishing House, 1973.
   TRINITY SUNDAY/DISCLOSED AS ONE: TRINITY SUNDAY

Benjamin Brody's Backyard Bag. Wezeman, Phyllis Vos and Colleen Aalsburg Wiessner. Illustrated by Christopher Raschka. Elgin, IL: Brethren Press, 1991.
   SECOND SUNDAY IN LENT/EMPOWERED TO SHARE: SECOND SUNDAY IN LENT

Does God Know How to Tie Shoes? Carlstrom, Nancy White and Lori McElrath-Eslick, Illustrator. Grand Rapids, MI: William B. Eerdmans Publishing Company, 1993.
   FATHER'S DAY/ANSWERED IN LOVE: FATHER'S DAY

Granddad's Prayers of the Earth. Wood, Douglas and P. J. Lynch, Illustrator. Cambridge, MA: Candlewick Press, 1999.
   ALL SAINTS' DAY/REMEMBERED BY HEART: ALL SAINTS' DAY

I'll Always Love You. Wilhelm, Hans. New York: Crown Publishers, Inc., 1985.
   VALENTINE'S DAY/SPOKEN WITH LOVE: VALENTINE'S DAY

In God's Name. Sasso, Sandy Eisenberg and Phoebe Stone, Illustrator. Woodstock, VT: Jewish Lights Publishing, 1994.
   REIGN OF CHRIST SUNDAY/NAMED BY ALL: REIGN OF CHRIST SUNDAY

Miss Fannie's Hat. Karon, Jan and Toni Goffe, Illustrator. Minneapolis, MN: Augsburg Fortress, 1998.
   FIFTH SUNDAY IN LENT/GIVEN WITH JOY: FIFTH SUNDAY IN LENT

Old Turtle. Wood, Douglas and Cheng-Khee Chee, Illustrator. Duluth, MN: Pfeifer-Hamilton Publishers, 1992.
   NEW YEAR'S DAY/ENVISIONED AS ONE: NEW YEAR'S DAY

People. Spier, Peter. New York: Doubleday, 1980.
   PENTECOST/BLESSED BY DIVERSITY: PENTECOST

Potluck. Shelby, Anne and Irene Trivas, Illustrator. New York: Orchard Books, 1991.
> INVITED TO SHARE: WORLD COMMUNION SUNDAY

Snowflake Bentley. Martin, Jacqueline Briggs and Mary Azarian, Illustrator. Boston: Houghton Mifflin Company, 1998.
> REVEALED FOR THE WORLD: FIRST SUNDAY IN ADVENT

Something from Nothing. Gilman, Phoebe. New York: Scholastic, 1993.
> REMEMBERED WITH GRATITUDE: THANKSGIVING DAY

Stellaluna. Cannon, Janell. San Diego, CA: Harcourt, Inc., 1993.
> NURTURED TO GROW: MOTHER'S DAY

Stone Soup. Brown, Marcia. New York: Atheneum Books, 1947.
> UNITED AS ONE: FOURTH OF JULY

Swimmy. Lionni, Leo. New York: Alfred A. Knopf, 1963.
> SHAPED FOR SERVICE: REFORMATION DAY

The Christmas Miracle of Jonathan Toomey. Wojciechowski, Susan and P. J. Lynch. Cambridge, MA: Candlewick Press, 1995.
> CRAFTED WITH CARE: FOURTH SUNDAY IN ADVENT

The Clown of God. dePaola, Tomie. San Diego: Harcourt Brace & Company, 1978.
> SHARED IN JOY: THIRD SUNDAY IN ADVENT

The Giving Tree. Silverstein, Shel. New York: Harper and Row, 1964.
> SIXTH SUNDAY IN LENT - OFFERED IN LOVE: PALM/PASSION SUNDAY

The Kissing Hand. Penn, Audrey and Ruth E. Harper and Nancy M. Leak, Illustrators. Washington, DC: Child & Family Press, 1993.
> ASSURED OF GOD'S PRESENCE: ASCENSION DAY

The Memory String. Bunting, Eve. New York: Clarion Books, 2000.
> STRENGTHENED BY MEMORIES: MEMORIAL DAY

The Quiltmaker's Gift. Brumbeau, Jeff and Gail de Marcken, Illustrator. Duluth, MN: Pfeifer-Hamilton Publishers, 2000.
> HUMBLED BY GENEROSITY: SECOND SUNDAY IN ADVENT

The Selfish Giant. Wilde, Oscar. Retold by Fiona Waters. Illustrated by Fabian Negrin. New York: Alfred A. Knopf, 1999.
> FREED TO LOVE: THIRD SUNDAY IN LENT

The Spyglass. Evans, Richard Paul and Jonathan Linton, Illustrator. New York: Simon & Schuster Books for Young Readers, 2000.
> JUSTIFIED BY FAITH: FOURTH SUNDAY IN LENT

The Tale of Three Trees. Hunt, Angela Elwell and Tim Jonke, Illustrator. Colorado Springs, CO: Lion Publishing, 1989.
> FULFILLED WITH PURPOSE: GOOD FRIDAY

The Very Hungry Caterpillar. Carle, Eric. New York: Philomel Books, 1983.
> AWAKENED TO NEW LIFE: EASTER SUNDAY

Three Wise Women. Hoffman, Mary and Lynne Russell, Illustrator. New York:

Phyllis Fogelman Books, 1999.

TOUCHED BY LIGHT: EPIPHANY

What Can I Give Him? Based on a Poem by Christina Rossetti. Gliori, Debi. New York: Holiday House, 1998.

BORN TO GIVE: CHRISTMAS

What If The Zebras Lost Their Stripes? Reitano, John and William Haines, Illustrator. Mahwah, NJ: Paulist Press, 1998.

REMINDED TO FORGIVE: FIRST SUNDAY IN LENT

Wilfrid Gordon McDonald Partridge. Fox, Mem and Julie Vivas, Illustrator. Brooklyn, NY: Kane/Miller, 1985.

HELPED TO REMEMBER: MAUNDY THURSDAY

You Are Special. Lucado, Max and Sergio Martinez, Illustrator. Wheaton, IL: Crossway Books, 1997.

HONORED AS IMPORTANT: LABOR DAY

Scripture Cross-References

Hebrew Scriptures

Joshua 4:1–7
  STRENGTHENED BY MEMORIES: MEMORIAL DAY –
  The Memory String

Psalm 34:8
  INVITED TO SHARE: WORLD COMMUNION SUNDAY – *Potluck*

Psalm 90:17
  HONORED AS IMPORTANT: LABOR DAY - *You Are Special*

Psalm 103:13
  ANSWERED IN LOVE: FATHER'S DAY –
  Does God Know How to Tie Shoes?

Psalm 135:13
  NAMED BY ALL: REIGN OF CHRIST SUNDAY – *In God's Name*

Proverbs 22:6
  NURTURED TO GROW: MOTHER'S DAY – *Stellaluna*

Isaiah 9:2b
  TOUCHED BY LIGHT: EPIPHANY – *Three Wise Women*

Isaiah 55:10, 11
  REVEALED FOR THE WORLD: FIRST SUNDAY IN ADVENT –
  Snowflake Bentley

Christian Scriptures

Luke 2:1–7
> BORN TO GIVE: CHRISTMAS – *What Can I Give Him?*

Luke 22:19–20
> HELPED TO REMEMBER: MAUNDY THURSDAY –
> *Wilfrid Gordon McDonald Partridge*

Luke 24:50–53
> ASSURED OF GOD'S PRESENCE: ASCENSION DAY –
> *The Kissing Hand*

John 3:17
> LENT: FULFILLED WITH PURPOSE: GOOD FRIDAY –
> *The Tale of Three Trees*

John 17:22–23
> UNITED AS ONE: FOURTH OF JULY – *Stone Soup*

Acts 2:1–14, 38–42
> BLESSED BY DIVERSITY: PENTECOST – *People*

Romans 3:21–24
> REMINDED TO FORGIVE: FIRST SUNDAY IN LENT –
> *What If The Zebras Lost Their Stripes?*

Romans 12:2
> SHAPED FOR SERVICE: REFORMATION DAY – *Swimmy*

1 Corinthians 15:51
> AWAKENED TO NEW LIFE: EASTER SUNDAY –
> *The Very Hungry Caterpillar*

2 Corinthians 5:7
> JUSTIFIED BY FAITH: FOURTH SUNDAY IN LENT – *The Spyglass*

2 Corinthians 8:9
> HUMBLED BY GENEROSITY: SECOND SUNDAY IN ADVENT –
> *The Quiltmaker's Gift*

2 Corinthians 9:15
>   SHARED IN JOY: THIRD SUNDAY IN ADVENT –
>   *The Clown of God*

2 Corinthians 13:13
>   REVEALED AS ONE: TRINITY SUNDAY –
>   *3 in 1 (A Picture of God)*

Ephesians 2:14
>   FREED TO LOVE: THIRD SUNDAY IN LENT – *The Selfish Giant*

Ephesians 5:2
>   OFFERED IN LOVE: PALM/PASSION SUNDAY,
>   SIXTH SUNDAY IN LENT – *The Giving Tree*

1 Thessalonians 5:18
>   REMEMBERED WITH GRATITUDE: THANKSGIVING DAY –
>   *Something from Nothing*

Hebrews 12:1
>   REMEMBERED BY HEART: ALL SAINTS' DAY –
>   *Granddad's Prayers of the Earth*

Hebrews 12:2
>   GIVEN WITH JOY: FIFTH SUNDAY IN LENT – *Miss Fannie's Hat*

1 Peter 2:21
>   EMPOWERED TO SHARE: SECOND SUNDAY IN LENT –
>   *Benjamin Brody's Backyard Bag*

1 John 4:7
>   SPOKEN WITH LOVE: VALENTINE'S DAY – *I'll Always Love You*

1 John 4:15
>   CRAFTED WITH CARE: FOURTH SUNDAY IN ADVENT –
>   *The Christmas Miracle of Jonathan Toomey*

Revelation 21:5
>   ENVISIONED AS ONE: NEW YEAR'S DAY – *Old Turtle*

Teaching Tool
Cross-References

Apple; Paring Knife
  Revealed as One: Trinity Sunday – *3 in 1 (A Picture of God)*
Baby Blanket
  Remembered with Gratitude: Thanksgiving Day –
  Something from Nothing
Basket containing egg, football, marionette, medal, and seashell
  Helped to Remember: Maundy Thursday –
  Wilfrid Gordon McDonald Partridge
Bat Finger Puppet
  Nurtured to Grow: Mother's Day – *Stellaluna*
Block of Wood
  Crafted with Care: Fourth Sunday in Advent –
  The Christmas Miracle of Jonathan Toomey
Book, Model, or Poster of the Lifecycle of a Butterfly
  Awakened to New Life: Easter Sunday –
  The Very Hungry Caterpillar
Bread (Loaf)
  Helped to Remember: Maundy Thursday –
  Wilfrid Gordon McDonald Partridge
Breadbasket
  Invited to Share: World Communion Sunday – *Potluck*
Buttons on a String
  Strengthened by Memories: Memorial Day –
  The Memory String
Calendar

Envisioned as One: New Year's Day – *Old Turtle*

Communion Cup

Helped to Remember: Maundy Thursday –
Wilfrid Gordon McDonald Partridge

Fabric or Paper, Black and White Striped

Reminded to Forgive: First Sunday in Lent –
What If The Zebras Lost Their Stripes?

Hat (Pink straw with pink roses)

Given With Joy: Fifth Sunday in Lent – *Miss Fannie's Hat*

Heart Ornament

Born to Give: Christmas – *What Can I Give Him?*

Heart-shaped Valentine Card

Spoken with Love: Valentine's Day – *I'll Always Love You*

Inflatable Fish

Shaped for Service: Reformation Day – *Swimmy*

Juggling Balls

Shared in Joy: Third Sunday in Advent – *The Clown of God*

Kaleidoscope

Blessed by Diversity: Pentecost – *People*

Lumber

Fulfilled with Purpose: Good Friday – *The Tale of Three Trees*

Mirror

Named by All: Reign of Christ Sunday – *In God's Name*

Palm Branches

Offered in Love: Palm/Passion Sunday – *The Giving Tree*

Paper Shopping Bag

Empowered to Share: Second Sunday in Lent –
Benjamin Brody's Backyard Bag

Patchwork Quilt

Humbled by Generosity: Second Sunday in Advent –
The Quiltmaker's Gift

Picture of Deceased Grandfather or Great-Grandfather

Remembered by Heart: All Saints' Day –

About the Authors

Phyllis Vos Wezeman

Phyllis Vos Wezeman is president of Active Learning Associates, Inc., and Director of Christian Nurture at First Presbyterian Church in South Bend, Indiana. Phyllis has served as adjunct faculty in the education department at Indiana University and the department of theology at the University of Notre Dame. She has taught at the Saint Petersburg (Russia) State University and the Shanghai (China) Teacher's University. Phyllis, who holds an M.S. in education from Indiana University, is a recipient of three "Distinguished Alumna Awards" and the Catholic Library Association's Aggiornamento Award. Author or coauthor of over 1,100 books and articles, Phyllis and her husband Ken have three children and three grandsons.

Anna L. Liechty

Anna Liechty is a National Board Certified teacher and chair of the English Department at Plymouth High School in Indiana. She has also worked as a religious education volunteer, teaching at all levels, directing Sunday morning and youth programming, consulting with congregations about their educational ministry, and writing a wide variety of religious education materials. She serves as vice president of Active Learning Associates, Inc. Anna lives in Plymouth, Indiana, with her husband Ron, a retired pastor. They have five children and ten grandchildren.

Other Books from The Pilgrim Press

Wipe the Tears
30 Children's Sermons on Death
Phyllis Vos Wezeman, Anna L. Liechty, and Kenneth R. Wezeman
ISBN 0-8298-1520-1/96 pages/paper/$10.00

Taste the Bread
30 Children's Sermons on Communion
Phyllis Vos Wezeman, Anna L. Liechty, and Kenneth R. Wezeman
ISBN 0-8298-1519-8/96 pages/paper/$10.00

Touch the Water
30 Children's Sermons on Baptism
Phyllis Vos Wezeman, Anna L. Liechty, Kenneth R. Wezeman
ISBN 0-8298-1518-X/112 pages/paper/$10.00

Planting Seeds of Faith
Virginia H. Loewen
ISBN 0-8298-1473-6/96 pages/paper/$10.00

Growing Seeds of Faith
Virginia H. Loewen
ISBN 0-8298-1488-4/96 pages/paper/$10.00

The Brown Bag
Jerry Marshall Jordan
ISBN 0-8298-0411-0/117 pages/paper/$9.95

Small Wonders
Sermons for Children
Glen E. Rainsley
ISBN 0-8298-1252-0/104 pages/paper/$12.95

Time with Our Children
Stories for Use in Worship, Year B
Dianne E. Deming
ISBN 0-8298-0952-X/182 pages/paper/$9.95

Time with Our Children
Stories for Use in Worship, Year C
Dianne E. Deming
ISBN 0-8298-0953-8/157 pages/paper/$9.95

To order these or any other books from The Pilgrim Press, call or write to:
The Pilgrim Press
700 Prospect Avenue East, Cleveland, Ohio 44115-1100
Phone orders: 1-800-537-3394 • Fax orders: 216-736-2206
Please include shipping charges of $4 for the first book and 75¢ for each additional book.
Or order from our Web sites at www.thepilgrimpress.com and www.ucpress.com.
Prices subject to change without notice.